DELIVERING THE GOODS

The LTCB International Library Trust

The LTCB (Long-Term Credit Bank of Japan) International Library Trust was established in July 2000, with the liquidated assets of the LTCB International Library Foundation, which was dissolved in the same year, to carry on the original mission of the Foundation which was stated by the founders of the Foundation as follows:

> The world is moving steadily toward a borderless economy and deepening international interdependence. Amid this globalization of economic activities, the Japanese economy is developing organic ties with the economies of individual nations throughout the world via trade, direct investment, overseas manufacturing activities, and the international movement of capital.
>
> As a result, interest in Japan's politics, economy, and society and in the concepts and values that lie behind Japan's socioeconomic activities is growing in many countries.
>
> However, the overseas introduction and dissemination of translations of works originally written in Japanese lags behind the growth of interest in Japan. Such works are not well known outside Japan. One main reason for this is that the high costs involved in translating and publishing materials written in Japanese hinder the undertaking of such activities on a commercial basis. It is extremely important to overcome this barrier to deepen and broaden mutual understanding.
>
> The LTCB International Library Foundation has been founded to address this pressing need. Its primary activity is to disseminate information on Japan in foreign countries through the translation of selected Japanese works on Japan's politics, economy, society, and culture into English and other languages and the publication and distribution of these translations. To commemorate the completion of the Long-Term Credit Bank of Japan, Ltd.'s new headquarters and its fortieth anniversary, LTCB has provided the LTCB International Library Foundation with an endowment.

In pursuing these objectives by way of publishing and distributing the English translations of books written by Japanese authors in the broad fields of Japanese politics, economy, society, and culture, the LTCB International Library Trust hopes to be able to contribute to enhancing international understanding and to the intellectual enrichment of the human community at large.

While the assets management of the LTCB International Library Trust is being handled by the Chuo Mitsui Trust and Banking Company, Ltd., the implementation of the publication project has been entrusted to the International House of Japan, Inc.

DELIVERING THE GOODS

*Entrepreneurship and Innovation
in a Japanese Corporation*

by

OGURA MASAO

translated by David Noble

 LTCB International Library Trust/International House of Japan

LTCB International Library Selection No.16

Transliteration of Foreign Words

The Hepburn system of romanization is used for Japanese terms, including the names of persons and places. Except for familiar place names, long vowels are indicated by macrons. The older Hepburn practice of using *m* instead of *n* before *p*, *b*, or *m* is followed. An apostrophe is used to distinguish syllable-final *n* from *n* at the beginning of a syllable.

Throughout this work, Japanese names are given in traditional order, surname first.

Yen-Dollar Exchange Rate, 1975–2002

Year	1975	1976	1977	1978	1979	1980	1981
Yen	296.787	296.552	268.510	210.442	219.140	226.741	220.536
Year	1982	1983	1984	1985	1986	1987	1988
Yen	249.077	237.512	237.522	238.536	168.520	144.637	128.152
Year	1989	1990	1991	1992	1993	1994	1995
Yen	137.964	144.792	134.707	126.651	111.198	102.208	94.060
Year	1996	1997	1998	1999	2000	2001	2002
Yen	108.779	120.991	130.905	113.907	107.765	121.529	125.388

Source: PACIFIC Exchange Rate Service, "Foreign Currency Units per 1 U.S. dollar, 1948–2002"
© by Prof. Werner Antweiler, University of British Columbia

English translation rights reserved by The International House of Japan, Inc. under contract with Ogura Masao and through the courtesy of Nikkei BP Sha.

© 2004 by The International House of Japan

First English edition published March 2004
by The International House of Japan
11-16, 5-chome, Minato-ku, Tokyo 106-0032, Japan
Tel: +81-3-3470-9059   Fax: +81-3-3470-3170

Printed in Japan

Contents

Preface

Takkyūbin. It scarcely seemed viable as a business plan, and was an audacious challenge to postal parcel delivery, but somehow, against all odds, it has grown and prospered.

Yamato Transport's Takkyūbin delivery service handled almost 780 million parcels in 1999, nearly two-and-a-half times the amount carried by the Japanese postal service. With a 37 percent share of the home parcel delivery market, it was well ahead of Nippon Express's Pelican service with 17 percent, and the postal service with 15 percent.

We launched Takkyūbin in February 1976. Up to that time, the only way to send small parcels was via the postal service. That's where we saw our chance to break into the market. The first year we handled only 1.7 million parcels compared to the 178.8 million carried by the postal service. Everyone thought our experiment was doomed to failure.

However, in the early 1980s we passed the break-even point and began turning a profit. Seeing this, more than thirty other companies jumped on the home parcel delivery bandwagon. The nation's children were all singing the Takkyūbin ad jingle, featuring our Black Cat mascot.

About that time I began to get a lot of requests from publishers to write a book about my experiences as president of Yamato Transport. But I turned them all down.

I'd seen too many cases in which a successful entrepreneur had published his reflections on management, only to have his company go down the drain not long after. I honestly believed that putting out a book would be a jinx that would bring misfortune to the company, so I kept my silence.

In June 1995 I stepped down as chairman of the board at Yamato Transport, and since that time have served as director of the Yamato Welfare Foundation, whose goal is assisting handicapped people to achieve greater personal autonomy and a higher level of participation in society. Since its establishment in 1993, the foundation has concentrated much of its work on support for a system of community workshops providing employment for people with disabilities.

Through my engagement with this work I was shocked to discover that the average monthly wage paid to handicapped people employed by these workshops was only ¥10,000 (less than a hundred dollars)! In this day and age, people were working for ¥10,000 a month—it was astonishing!

How could this be? Largely it seemed to stem from the fact that the people running the workshops, though passionately committed to the welfare of people with disabilities, really knew next to nothing about business management.

As I mused on this, it occurred to me that while I myself knew next to nothing about social welfare, I did have forty-two years of managerial experience at Yamato Transport. Perhaps, by sharing that experience, I could put it to work for the workshops. So for three years, from 1996 to 1998, I offered annual "Community Workshop Power-Up Seminars" at a dozen or so places across the country. About 1,400 people attended, and seem to have found the talks quite useful.

These seminars were one of the reasons I decided to write this book. It has now been four years since I retired as an officer of Yamato Transport. Since I am no longer actively involved in running the company, I see no reason to worry any longer about the jinx. My memory of my years of active service with the company are beginning to fade. Looking back on it, in my years as an entrepreneur I made many decisions that I never explained in detail to my employees. So it seemed there might be some value in talking about why I thought and behaved as I did while I was president of the company.

This was what led me to set about writing this book. It is my first book, and I expect it will be my last—a once in a lifetime thing. This is my only experience with making something and selling it. All I know is the transport industry, and I wonder sometimes whether what I have to say will be useful to a broader audience.

I have no interest in writing a success story. All I have tried to do is write honestly about what went on in my poor head all these years.

Ogura Masao

Prologue:
Goodbye Mitsukoshi, Hello Takkyūbin!

It was the evening of March 1, 1979. The main banquet hall at Happō-en in the Shirokane area of Tokyo was filled with the happy clamor of more than two hundred employees of the Mitsukoshi office of Yamato Transport Co., Ltd.

On the last day of February Yamato Transport had formally ended its relationship as shipper for Mitsukoshi, Ltd., then Japan's largest department store group. As a result, our Mitsukoshi office was being eliminated, and the Happō-en event was a farewell party for its staff.

Ordinarily, the demise of a long-familiar workplace would result in a rather glum gathering, but the faces of the employees were cheerful, and the talk was lively.

Mitsukoshi had been Yamato Transport's most valuable client.

Yamato Transport opened for business in November 1919 with a fleet of four trucks, but was hit hard by the depression that began the following March. For a time the very existence of the company was in question. But Yamato was able to ride out this crisis thanks to a contract it signed in 1923 with Mitsukoshi Dry Goods (forerunner of Mitsukoshi Department Store) to deliver the company's goods within the city of Tokyo.

Yamato Transport's founder, Ogura Yasuomi, treated Mitsukoshi from the beginning as a privileged client, and for its part, Mitsukoshi valued Yamato as the mainstay of its distribution service. Twice a year, just before the busy midsummer and year-end gift-giving seasons *(chūgen* and *seibo),* it was customary for the head of Mitsukoshi's main store to invite the manager of Yamato's Mitsukoshi office to a luncheon at which the latter was encouraged to provide the best delivery service possible at these crucial times of year. The relationship of solidarity and trust between the two firms seemed unshakable.

However, with the appointment of Okada Shigeru as president of Mitsukoshi in 1972, the situation drastically altered.

Okada's management priorities could be summed up in one word: sales. He constantly and imperiously commanded his employees to start using their heads and produce better sales figures—by any means necessary.

Relations with Mitsukoshi's business allies also came under the sway of Okada's total obsession with sales. Okada liked to say that these business associates were Mitsukoshi customers, too—and ones who were in no position to complain about a hard sell.

Yamato Transport was no exception. The company was pressured into buying expensive furniture and clocks from Mitsukoshi, as well as paintings imported from Russia, and even land for vacation retreats. I myself was strong-armed into joining five of Okada's lavish overseas excursions, beginning with a trip to Versailles.

The year Okada became president of Mitsukoshi, the store celebrated its three-hundredth anniversary with a commemorative ceremony. As a business associate of better than fifty years standing, Yamato Transport was also to be honored. When we delivered the formal card declaring our intention of presenting Mitsukoshi with three hundred bottles of saké for the celebration, we were told not to bother—just to add the price of the saké to our payables to Mitsukoshi as part of retail sales, so it would look as if we had bought the saké at their store! That's not all. Every year Mitsukoshi gave away calendars to its clients; illustrated by first-class artists, they were quite popular items. In the old days, the head of the shipping department would always give us a few copies if asked. Then, one year, we were presented with twenty or thirty of the calendars without even asking. The Yamato employee receiving them said, "My, how generous of you!" to the Mitsukoshi rep, who startled him by replying, "Oh no, from now on we're charging for them." An even bigger surprise came a few years later, when Mitsukoshi published an expensive coffee-table collection of the paintings that had been featured in its calendars—and pressured Yamato to buy it. Later I was told that all of these were ideas of Okada's.

Okada also thought of himself as something of a man of the arts, one result of which was a film called *Burning Autumn,* which he produced. All well and good, except that Yamato Transport was forced to buying a thousand reserved-seat tickets when it opened.

I could cite many more examples like these, yet there was little to do other than write them off as ancillary costs of doing business in this impure world. But what I could not stomach was the outrageous treatment Yamato was subjected to time and again in the context of the business relationship itself.

In October 1974, as its own performance began to slump, Mitsukoshi adopted the following measures by order of President Okada:

1. Lowering the rates Mitsukoshi would pay for shipping
2. Collection of parking fees at Mitsukoshi distribution centers from trucks owned by Yamato Transport, even though they were used exclusively for Mitsukoshi deliveries
3. Collection of office-use fees from the Yamato Transport employees stationed within Mitsukoshi's company facilities

The latter two policies in particular seemed to violate the rules of common sense, but we were forced to accept them, on the condition that they were to be temporary measures, remaining in force only until Mitsukoshi recovered from its difficulties.

Then, in 1976, as part of an effort to streamline operations, Mitsukoshi merged its distribution centers at Itabashi and Fukagawa into a single Fukagawa facility, and twisted Yamato Transport's arm until we signed a lease on the disused Itabashi center—to the tune of ¥66 million a year.

As a result of all of this, the financial situation of Yamato's Mitsukoshi office went into a steep decline after 1976, racking up annual deficits of more than ¥100 million.

Meanwhile, Mitsukoshi's fortunes recovered, to the point that in the first quarter of 1978 the company posted pretax profits of more than ¥10 trillion. In light of this, we approached them about increasing our shipping rates, but they seemed unwilling to negotiate in good faith.

That was when I made up my mind.

In light of our fifty-year relationship and the obligations incurred, it might seem that tearing up our contract with Mitsukoshi was not a good business move. But as an entrepreneur, I could not let Yamato's huge deficits continue unchecked.

Naturally, if it had just been a matter of the Mitsukoshi office running in the red for a while, I would probably never have contemplated reevaluating our contract with such a well-established client. Sometimes business is good; sometimes it's bad. However, I could no longer tolerate Okada's methods —I was totally fed up with trying to work with him.

After deliberating on the matter with our board of directors, in November 1978 I went to Tsuda Kōji, managing director of Mitsukoshi's flagship store, and informed him of our intent to dissolve our distribution contract with Mitsukoshi as of the end of February 1979. I promised that Yamato would fulfill its responsibilities to Mitsukoshi during the year-end gift-giving period so critical to department stores, but that after February we could not continue our relationship. Brushing off his attempts to dissuade me, I returned to my office.

So sayonara to our biggest client. But there was another important factor that made it possible for me to make such a decision.

A totally new business of ours—a home express delivery service we had named Takkyūbin—had taken off quite rapidly. From its launch in 1976, Takkyūbin quickly dissolved any initial doubts about its viability by showing steady and consistent growth, from 1.7 million deliveries in the first fiscal year to 5.4 million in 1977, and over 10 million in 1978.

It was the prospect of Takkyūbin as the new pillar of our operations that allowed me not to hesitate over the critical decision to part company with our most important client.

The maturing of the Takkyūbin business also meant that the parting with Mitsukoshi could be accomplished without undue concern on the part of Yamato Transport's employees. I had informed the labor union in advance of this plan, and they approved it wholeheartedly, though not without adding some stiff demands of their own regarding job placement and treatment of employees who would be affected by the decision. I told them not to worry, winning their approval by promising that, based on the employees' own wishes, I would either place them in our distribution operations for other department stores, or in the Takkyūbin service.

Later, other department stores asked me if I had gotten sick of department store delivery work now that Takkyūbin was up and running, but I assured them that this was impossible, telling them that department store distribution and express delivery services were not only compatible, they were synergistic, and that far from abandoning our department-store work, I wanted to strengthen it. It was just that I had gotten fed up with Okada.

Severing our relationship with Mitsukoshi—or, more to the point, with Okada—was a breath of fresh air for everyone at Yamato Transport, and there was an upsurge of enthusiasm for making Takkyūbin a success.

Right about the time we were closing out our accounts with Mitsukoshi, Ogura Yasuomi, my father and the founder of Yamato Transport, passed away. It was January 15, 1979, and he was eighty-nine years old. It was a very emotional time for me.

The passing of our founder and the parting with Mitsukoshi marked the end of an era for Yamato Transport. A new day was dawning, and the banquet at Happō-en was, in a sense, a celebration of this new beginning— powered by our Takkyūbin operations.

PART ONE
Gyūdon and Manhattan

Y amato Transport, founded in the Taishō era (1912–25), had succeeded in becoming Japan's largest trucking company by the eve of World War II, largely on the strength of its short-haul services. But the company was slow to move into the long-distance trucking sector that sprang up along with the postwar recovery of Japanese industry, and soon found itself in trouble. Founder Ogura Yasuomi's earlier experience of success had become a liability. Diversification was seized upon as the way out of the dilemma, but none of the new enterprises went anywhere, and as revenue from the core business of commercial freight transport declined, the company faced a serious crisis.

Meanwhile, my involvement in Yamato's management began in the mid-1950s, and from business seminars and other sources I absorbed the knowledge I would need as an entrepreneur: I studied the management techniques of American companies and manufacturing firms, the history of the transportation revolution, and techniques for reading the market. When I took office as president of Yamato Transport, I was convinced we could ride out the crisis by shifting our target from commercial freight transport to the consumer parcel-delivery market, and by rejecting diversification in favor of concentrating all our efforts on a single service. One of my inspirations was Yoshinoya, the restaurant chain that made its fortune on a single menu item—the humble dish of stewed beef over rice known as gyūdon. But the home delivery market had been monopolized to that point by the Japanese postal service, because of the major difficulties involved in achieving efficient pickup and delivery. How were we going to break into it? My theory was that if we could put together a nationwide network we would succeed, and when I saw UPS delivery trucks cruising the streets of Manhattan, I knew I was right.

The Background to Takkyūbin

What led me to launch Takkyūbin? In order to explain that I must first touch on the management of Yamato Transport under my father, Ogura Yasuomi, founder of the company.

Successful entrepreneurs often become prisoners of their past successes, charting a mistaken path for their companies because they misread changes in the business environment. My father was a case in point. Before the war, he built Yamato Transport into Japan's biggest trucking company on the basis of short-haul lines. But after the war, as the market changed, his earlier prior success became an obstacle to Yamato's entry into long-distance freight transport, and the company fell into a managerial crisis.

Yamato's entry into a completely new market—express parcel delivery— was a last-ditch effort to breathe life back into a dying company.

In this chapter, I will take a brief look at the history that brought Yamato Transport to this critical juncture.

Prewar Japan's Biggest Trucking Company

Yamato Transport opened for business on November 29, 1919, with a fleet of 4 trucks and main offices in Kobikichō in Tokyo's Kyōbashi Ward (now Ginza Sanchōme). Since there were only 240 trucks in the entire country at the time, it could truly be called a pioneering effort.

Ogura Yasuomi launched Yamato Transport on his thirtieth birthday (he was born in Kyōbashi in 1889). A successful greengrocer at age twenty-five, he witnessed the economic boom that followed World War I, became convinced that the automotive age was dawning, and after considerable research, decided to start a trucking company.

He began with ¥100,000 of capital, and from the beginning Yamato took the form of a joint-stock company. In addition to the company president, there were fifteen employees (seven office clerks and eight drivers), but in his hiring of a Keio University graduate in 1923, one can already see Yasuomi's efforts to adopt the techniques of modern management. In 1924 he had the drivers begin wearing uniforms, and the smartness of their appearance—policeman's caps, green twill collars, and jodhpurs—was a genuine innovation that succeeded in lending an air of reliability to the company.

Yamato Transport grew steadily, making a name for itself with the transport of fresh seafood, a market in which time was of the essence, and by concluding a valuable contract with Mitsukoshi for delivery of its goods within the city of Tokyo. The Great Kantō Earthquake of 1923, which devastated Tokyo and Yokohama, created a skyrocketing demand for transport during the period of reconstruction that followed, and this served as an additional spur to the company's growth.

An even more important impetus behind the company's expansion was Yasuomi's visit to Europe. In 1927 he attended the World Congress on Automotive Transport, held in London, and afterward visited the head offices of Carter Paterson, Ltd., where he was to learn a great deal.

Carter Paterson ran transport services within a network centered on London but reaching as far as Birmingham and Glasgow—150 miles east to west, 120 miles north to south. Especially noteworthy was the fact that their regularly scheduled trucks offered completely integrated door-to-door service, handling pickup, transport, and delivery. "This Carter Paterson system left a deep impression on me," Yasuomi later recalled. "I thought: I'm going to introduce this system when I get back to Japan, and get a head start on the competition."

Yasuomi began to achieve this goal within two years of returning home. In 1929 he began running regularly scheduled trucks on a route between Tokyo and Odawara, carrying parcels and light freight for a variety of companies. He then steadily expanded his network, running routes from Tokyo to Hachiōji, Takasaki, Utsunomiya, Mito, and Chiba. By 1935 he had succeeded in building a network covering the entire Kantō region, with a total length of 1,801 kilometers, comprised of 14 separate routes served by 51 local offices, a fleet of 151 trucks, and 500 employees. Yamato Transport had grown into a major company.

If we look at the numbers for 1945, Yamato Transport had total sales of ¥3.92 million, pretax profits of ¥490,000, and an operating profit ratio of 12.5 percent. Figures like these made its position indisputable as the number-one trucking company in Japan.

Much of the credit for Yamato's growth during the prewar period can be attributed to Yasuomi's innovative thinking and entrepreneurial skill. His use of the name "Yamato Lines" for his network of regular-route trucks, establishing it in the mind of the public as a byword for handy and convenient service; his adoption from the outset of the joint-stock model of corporate organization; his success at winning consumer trust with his innovatively uniformed drivers; his monthly management meetings; the fact that as early as 1931 Yamato was already publishing a company news-letter—all of these policies are testimony to Yasuomi's efforts at modern, rational management of the company, as well as to his lively imagination and skill at implementing his ideas.

However, in the 1940s, as World War II dragged on and raw materials such as gasoline became increasingly scarce, truck transport over distances of more than fifty kilometers was prohibited, and the trucking industry shifted its efforts to meeting the demand for military transport. Yamato Transport had no choice but to reduce its network and close many of its branch offices, and it greeted the end of the war in a greatly weakened condition.

The Dangers of Past Success—Yamato Fails at Long-Range Freight Transport
As soon as the war ended, Yamato Transport was back in business. Greeting the new era appropriately by working for the Occupation forces, the company soon began turning a profit. Moreover, with the opening of Japan National Railways freight stations to private-sector business, Yamato tried its hand at the forwarding business. In this case, forwarding meant the "off-rail" end of the JNR freight service—in other words, the receiving, trans-shipping, and delivery of goods between the railway stations and either the shipper or recipient, including contracting for the loading and unloading of the railway freight cars. Such work required a license, and during the war it had been the monopoly of Nippon Express Company, Ltd. (better known as Nittsū). After the war, the breakup of monopolies was a key policy of the Occupation, and at each freight station, several competing firms were permitted to newly enter this business. Yamato received licenses to operate at Shiodome, Akihabara, and Iidamachi stations (and later at Sumidagawa station). Yet even with this new line of business, the mainstay of Yamato

Transport continued to be its regular truck routes, and the company poured its energies into reestablishing the Yamato Lines network it had built up in the prewar period.

It was at exactly this point that I entered the company.

In 1943, at the height of World War II, I graduated from the old First Higher School and entered Tokyo Imperial University in the department of economics. But my life as a student came to an abrupt end—in 1944 I became a part of the general student mobilization that took place at that time, and in October of that year I was sent to the Reserve Officers Training School in Kurume on the island of Kyūshū. In June 1945, I was posted as an officer to a detached infantry battalion in Gamagōri in Aichi Prefecture, and there, in August, learned of the war's end.

With the war over, I was demobilized and returned to university, but it was difficult to enjoy student life in the midst of the terrible food shortages. With some fellow students from the Applied Sciences division and some tennis buddies from my Higher School days, I began manufacturing the artificial sweetener saccharin—and in the meantime graduated from university, in September 1947.

Saccharin made money. We started out in a shed behind the house of one of my friends, but in less than a year we had bought a 1400-square-foot factory in Suginami Ward and had incorporated as a joint-stock company.

However, I couldn't explore life's byways forever. From my student days I'd always assumed I would work for father's company, and a year after graduation, in September 1948, I joined Yamato Transport.

Only a few months later, I was suddenly forced to take a leave of absence from work. I had contracted tuberculosis.

The next two years were spent in the hospital in a constant battle with the disease. It was a tough time, but TB was often fatal in those days, and I had to count myself fortunate simply for surviving. But I left the hospital in no condition to go back to work. In fact, I struggled through another two and a half years of recuperation at home before I recovered the strength the disease had robbed from me. For someone in their twenties, in the prime of their working life, this four-and-a-half-year blank seemed an eternity.

I finally returned to work at Yamato Transport in November 1953, and the following July I was seconded to an affiliated company, Shizuoka Transport. It was a small company, and precisely because of that, I had to keep an eye on everything from personnel management to on-site work procedures. It was a valuable opportunity for me to learn the ABCs of managing a freight trucking company. In September 1956 I was recalled from this position to become head of the department store unit of Yamato Transport. I was thirty-one years old.

In the decade since the end of the war, the trucking industry in Japan had gone through some major changes. Particularly noteworthy was the rise of companies from western Japan such as Seino Transportation and Nippon Transport. The Tokaidō Expressway from Tokyo to Osaka was known as the "Golden Route," and became the scene of intense competition between the major freight lines. Before the war such long-distance freight transport was regarded as virtually the exclusive province of the railways. Why did the trucking industry begin to make inroads into it?

The first reason was the improvement of the road system. The tempo was excruciatingly slow, but after the war the network of properly paved roads gradually expanded. The second reason was that conversion of military trucks to civilian use had resulted in a dramatic improvement in performance.

But there was an even more important reason than either of these. The demand for freight transport itself had changed significantly. After the war, the desperate struggle of Japan's manufacturing sector to kick-start the economy resulted in a flood of home appliances and other manufactured goods from producers to consumers. As a result, there was explosive growth in the demand for transport from the industrial zones of the Kansai region to the Tokyo consumer market.

The railroads had dominated long-range freight transport up to this point, but a number of disadvantages gradually became apparent. Rail transport, as long as it stayed on the rails, was fast—70 kilometers an hour or faster. But it took a lot of time before the goods ever left the station. Three or four hours were required to load the cars and couple them into trains going to the same destinations. Because of this, the goods had to be delivered to the freight yards well in advance of the estimated time of departure. If they arrived late, they wouldn't ship until the next day's train.

Here trucks had a real advantage over the rails. Trucks loaded directly at the factory, and could depart at any time. Because of this, even though they might average only 30 kilometers an hour, their door-to-door times were competitive with the railways. Moreover, with the greater volume of shipping after the war, trucks could travel fully loaded, gradually reducing their freight rates and making clients happy.

In this way, trucking began to steal center stage from the railways in the long-range freight industry. Right after the war, the tipping point between the volume of freight traveling by rail and that traveling by truck came at one hundred kilometers (the distance from Tokyo to Shizuoka). Before long this expanded to four hundred kilometers (Tokyo to Nagoya), and then to five hundred kilometers (Tokyo to Osaka).

So the market was undergoing major changes. Despite this fact, Yamato Transport hunkered down amid its established local lines in the Kantō region. This was because Yasuomi, the company president, remained absolutely convinced that the domain of trucking was anything under a hundred kilometers, and that anything over that belonged to the railroads. I was at the forefront of a group of younger company executives who pleaded with him to take the company into the long-range freight market, but Yasuomi stubbornly refused to permit this.

It is true that in the prewar era, Yamato succeeded because Yasuomi stuck to his guns and concentrated exclusively on local transport. However, as I have just recounted, the market for truck transport had dramatically altered.

"If we go on like this, we are going to be left behind." My arguments, and the strength of internal company opinion, eventually got through to Yasuomi, who gave his blessing to entering the competition on the Tokaidō route.

In January 1957 we applied for a license to operate on the Tokyo–Osaka route, which we received in November 1959. I, who had argued so strongly for getting into long-range freight, was made vice-president in charge of operations and a member of the board of directors, and sent to Osaka to lead the team working to develop a new client base there.

In March 1960 our Osaka branch office finally opened for business—a mere five years behind our competitors.

That five-year gap hurt us badly. When I went on the round of visits expected of a newly established company, I found to my dismay that our major prospective clients had already established relationships with our competitors, and there wasn't much business left for us.

Yasuomi was without a doubt an excellent businessman. But no matter how excellent a businessman one may be, the experience of past success can become a major obstacle to developing new enterprises in response to changing times—a lesson never more clearly felt than at that time.

Some Profit—Others Don't

We had finally made our long-awaited debut on the Tokaidō route, but now found we couldn't assemble the freight we needed to carry. This was a problem. On long-distance runs like this, we couldn't just send the trucks back to Tokyo empty—that wouldn't pay at all. We absolutely had to do something to find the necessary freight.

In any case, I'd been appointed head of operations with the goal of signing up the sort of big shippers that would make our long-range shipping efforts feasible, so I poured all my energy into efforts to win new clients.

From the mid-1950s to the mid-60s, the Japanese economy grew enormously. Industrial complexes were being built everywhere, and communities were doing everything they could to attract industry. "Towering smokestacks" became a kind of catch phrase for the construction of new factories, and I spurred the sales staff to go out and get the owners of those smokestacks as our clients. As a result, Yamato Transport's gross sales showed modest growth.

But we were not out of the woods yet. Our current profits were gradually declining.

In 1960 our operating profit on sales was 3.1 percent; by 1965 it had fallen to 1.7 percent. We'd thought we might have to sacrifice a bit of our profit margin as we shifted our emphasis to bulk freight for large corporate clients, but such a drop was quite unanticipated. We had to do something to rectify this.

I instructed our sales reps to turn down small shipments, as they were just as much trouble and less cost-effective. I had no idea at the time how big a mistake this would turn out to be.

As Yamato struggled to increase its profitability, Seino Transportation and the other Kansai firms were prospering.

I couldn't understand this. If we'd been in the midst of a recession, and no one in the industry was making money, then the drop in our profitability would have made some kind of sense. But this was Japan's era of high economic growth, and our competitors were making a killing. If you looked at the profit margins, Seino and the others were doing much better than we were. It was pathetic.

Other companies were raking it in—why couldn't we?

The first thing to consider was personnel costs. Our competitors were all based outside Tokyo, while we were headquartered there and paid higher wages as a result. On average, our employees were being paid ¥5,000 a month more than our competitors paid theirs.

But there was a bigger reason. At the time, some below-market discounting of freight rates to secure major clients was going on—but our competitors faced similar challenges, so it was unlikely that they were getting higher rates than we were, especially since trucking rates were regulated, with firms throughout the country using rate sheets approved by the Ministry of Transport.

Why were we the only ones not making money? As an entrepreneur, and an executive, this bothered me intensely and I had to get to the bottom of it. I racked my brains for quite some time, and then the answer suddenly came to me.

The system for setting trucking rates was, in principle, one of decreasing charges relative to distance and weight. In other words, the further the freight had to be hauled and the heavier it was, the lower the per-unit cost.

With regard to distance, the situation was the same for every company—the distance between Tokyo and Osaka didn't vary. But weight was another matter. Even trucks of the same size could be loaded differently by different companies. Given the system of decreasing charges by weight, you made less revenue on heavy cargo and more on light cargo.

Let me explain this in greater detail. Rates were computed on the basis of the individual shipment. The average contract shipment on Japanese trucking lines was 211 kilograms, or approximately 8.8 cardboard boxes holding 24 kilos apiece. In other words, a "heavy cargo" is not a matter of weight alone, but of the number of units making up the shipment.

With this in mind, I researched our rates on the Tokyo–Osaka route. I don't have the old figures readily to hand, so I will try to recap the calculations I did at that time, using an authorized rate sheet from 1974.

Let's start by assuming that we have a 50-unit shipment in which the units weigh 24 kilos each, for a total of 1200 kilos, and that the shipping rate for this is ¥11,000, or ¥220 per unit. However, the actual charge to a major shipper is discounted by 10 percent from the rate sheet, which means cutting ¥20 from the unit rate, leaving us with ¥200 per unit. By contrast, a 5-unit shipment totaling 120 kilos has a shipping rate of ¥1500, or ¥300 per unit.

You no doubt see where this leads. The unit rate for a 5-unit shipment is one and a half times the unit rate for a 50-unit shipment. By this reckoning, small-lot shipments are obviously much bigger moneymakers.

I was shocked. I immediately checked Yamato's records for long-distance freight shipments. The vast majority were 50-unit shipments or larger. Shipments of fewer than 10 units amounted to less than 10 percent of the total. What was the situation with our competitors? I had to find out. But the figures I wanted probably didn't exist—and even if they did, my rivals were not going to share them with me.

What could I do? On my next visit to Osaka, I did a bit of snooping outside the depots of our major rivals. As the drivers unloaded their trucks, they would group all the pieces from the same shipment together on the dock, waiting until the shipment was complete before moving it to its designated area. Thus, by watching the unloading process, you could get a pretty good idea of the size of the shipments that were being handled.

My observations told me that the companies with profit margins of better than 7 percent were grouping almost all their cargo in shipments of 5 units or less. Companies with 5-percent profits were using shipments of 10 units or less. And Yamato was routinely assembling shipments of about 50 units. No wonder our profit margin was so low! What a mistake it had been to base our strategy on refusing small-lot shipments in favor of large ones! The other companies were also moving large shipments, but what this had completely hidden from me was the huge volume of small-lot shipping they were doing.

At the time, the rate for a single-unit shipment on the Tokyo–Osaka route was ¥700. The standard freight capacity of a large truck was ten (metric) tons. If the average loaded weight of a standard cardboard shipping container was 24 kilos, then a truck should hold about 400 units. If the truck were loaded with 50-unit lots, according to my previous calculations the per-unit rate would be ¥200, making the revenue from the 400-unit load come out to ¥80,000. But if the same truck were filled with single-unit lots, then the math was ¥700 times 400 units, for a total of ¥280,000 worth of revenue!

It took a lot of time and effort to assemble cargos made up of single-unit shipments. But if rates like this could be charged, then it was still attractive from a business perspective. In fact, the calculations I did at this time were in the back of my mind when I later began to think about starting the Takkyūbin operation.

But back to our story. I gave an urgent order to our staff to assemble small-lot shipments. However, many of the shippers wanted nothing to do with us. They were upset that we'd refused their small shipments before as being too much trouble, and yet were now coming around and asking for their business. It would have been better if we had just raised our rates and let the shippers decide not to ship with us—our refusal to do business with them had hurt their pride. I regretted how clumsily I had handled this, but there was no use crying over spilt milk.

Virtuous Circles and Vicious Circles

In any industry with a great discrepancy in market share, you sometimes hear a company described as "standing head and shoulders above the rest" when the pecking order is being discussed. At that time, no one company was clearly standing head and shoulders above the rest in the trucking business, but a handful of companies were rapidly increasing market share, while a host of others were not. Yamato Transport, with its long history and diversified operations, was not regarded as one of the losers, but because I felt our failures in the long-range freight market so acutely, I privately thought we were quite typical of the firms that were going nowhere.

You have two companies, both doing the same work. One has a large and growing share of the market; the other is making no progress at all. Wherein lies the difference?

Think of the beer industry in Japan, which was once dominated by three companies. The top company had 60 percent of the market, the other two about 20 percent apiece. In other words, the top firm had a three to one advantage over each of its competitors. It could spend three times as much on advertising as either of its rivals, and since it was also likely to offer deeper discounts to retailers, it would enjoy better sales even with similar marketing efforts. Materials costs, though probably not half of what the others were paying, were certainly much lower due to economies of scale. If you look at it in this way, it is clear that the company with the largest market share is going to keep growing, while its rivals, as long as they follow the same path, are going to have a pretty difficult time catching up.

Yamato Transport was a case in point. In 1959, when I became vice-president in charge of operations, our truck terminal in the Fukagawa district of Tokyo was a decrepit wooden building, with holes in the floor, that wouldn't allow the use of forklifts. We were capitalized at ¥100 million, and so weak financially we couldn't afford to put anything into capital improvements. Loading and unloading had to be done with handcarts, which was not very efficient.

On the other hand, Seino Transportation had built a huge new concrete truck terminal in Nagoya. Their productivity increased, so their service was better; shippers trusted them, so their revenues and profits grew. They were in good financial shape, so they were able to invest in facilities and equipment, and their labor-management relations were also amicable.

In other words, Yamato suffered within a vicious circle, while Seino enjoyed a virtuous one. Inadequate capital, finances riddled with debt, old and inefficient facilities, low productivity, friction between labor and management, stalled revenues, falling profits—these had become mutually reinforcing causes and effects that were paralyzing the company. My head ached every day as I struggled to come up with some way to break out of this vicious circle. And yet I knew that neither vicious nor virtuous circles were built in a day. They are the result of many years, of decades.

So, what could lead us into a virtuous circle?

One fundamental condition was hard work. If you are running a shop, this means you open an hour earlier than your neighbor, and close an hour later. A trucking company is no different. Our regionally-based competitors were getting their employees to work harder than ours. Based as we were in Tokyo, where the labor unions were strong, we couldn't compel our employees to work longer hours.

Sometimes clever advertising can be the start of a virtuous circle for a company. I'm told that Art Moving Center, a successful moving company, chose its name because it put them in the A's in the Yellow Pages. They followed this up by getting a phone number ending in 0123, featured this prominently in their commercials and collateral advertising, made a name for themselves, and kicked off a remarkable surge in the company's growth.

Many companies start their cycle of success with the quality of their product. In fact, one might say this is the orthodox route. Higuchi Kōtarō, who left Sumitomo Bank to enter a completely different field of business as president of Asahi Beer, began by making a point about the freshness of his product—by having all of the company's beer that was more than a week old dumped in the river! Not long after, Asahi had a major hit with its Super Dry beer and the famous commercial "It's got bite—and body."

Where was Yamato Transport going to find the start of its virtuous circle? After a lot of thought, I decided: let's begin by doing something about labor productivity.

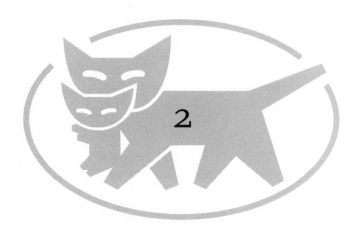

2

I Go Back to School

Before developing Takkyūbin, I spent a considerable period of time absorbing a wealth of information from seminars and lectures and applying it, in a process of trial and error, to my work as a manager.

In the late 1950s and early 1960s, when I became involved in the management of Yamato Transport, business seminars were being given all over Japan. These seminars were where I was first exposed to American management techniques and management of secondary industry, became aware of the necessity of increasing labor productivity as a step towards better management, and began thinking about how to apply what I had learned to the trucking business. In the late 60s and 70s I attended lectures on distribution and related fields, came to understand the difference between secondary and tertiary industries, and became convinced of the importance of restructuring the way goods were distributed. And in the years since launching Takkyūbin in 1976, I have continued to attend lectures, where I have acquired some of the concepts of marketing, types of operation, and participatory management that are directly reflected in Yamato's current management style.

What have I gained as a result of attending all these seminars and lectures? A conviction that management means thinking things through for yourself—and that this commitment to thought is of critical importance.

Improving Productivity

Increasing labor productivity—that was to be the first step towards Yamato's virtuous circle. But thinking it was one thing: how could we do it?

It was a seminar that helped show me the way.

The postwar recovery of the Japanese economy was proceeding at a rapid pace. To promote this recovery, leaders of Japanese industry organized a number of study tours of U.S. industries. The object was to discover the secret of America's high productivity. At home in Japan as well, seminars on productivity were being held in many parts of the country.

This was a time when the wages of American workers were several times higher than those of the Japanese; a time when virtually no Japanese owned their own cars, while there was one in every American garage. I was envious of this myself. And somehow American corporations were turning out internationally competitive, inexpensive products—despite high personnel costs—and were prospering as a result. I simply couldn't understand it.

So I went to seminars at every opportunity. At the seminars we were taught that the secret of American economic growth was high productivity, and that high productivity derived from increases in labor productivity brought about by increasing per-worker capital investment and thus increasing operating rates.

The shipping business is a classic example of a labor-intensive industry. Since personnel costs account for approximately 60 percent of total costs, increasing labor productivity is an essential condition for rationalizing operating expenses. Appointed vice-president for operations in 1959 at the age of thirty-four, I was intent on modernizing truck transport, and soon began putting into practice the things I had learned from the seminars on increasing productivity.

My first move was to shift our fleet towards larger trucks. At the time, the largest cargo capacity for standard trucks was eight tons. On the other hand, there were tractor-trailer rigs that could increase the cargo capacity to twelve tons. I stopped our purchases of standard trucks and ordered the fleet converted to tractor-trailers. This was in 1965, the year after the Tokyo Olympics.

But I had another reason—the real reason—for introducing tractor-trailer rigs. Trucks make money hauling freight. When they are loading and unloading, they are not hauling; when they are hauling, they cannot be loaded or unloaded. So even if you kept a truck operating twenty-four hours a day, in reality it would be operating productively only about half the time. From the standpoint of productivity theory, this was irrational.

Hence the beauty of the tractor-trailer system. The idea was to buy three trailers for each tractor. One trailer would be at each terminus being unloaded and loaded, while the tractor pulled the loaded third trailer on the route between the two terminuses. That way, with changes of drivers, the equipment could be put to productive use twenty-four hours a day.

In 1965 Yamato purchased its first team (one tractor, three trailers) and began the shift towards the tractor-trailer system. Actual operations began in 1966 on the Tokyo–Mito and Tokyo–Takasaki routes. By 1975 Yamato had fifty-five of these teams in operation.

In addition to increasing the operating rate of our fleet by introducing the tractor-trailer system, I introduced a number of innovations intended to increase the productivity of our employees. The first was the "relay" system we adopted in 1967 on our freight lines.

The normal work pattern on a long-distance run, like the Tokyo–Osaka route, would be for the driver to begin work in the evening, load his truck, and depart Tokyo about 9:00 PM. Arriving in Osaka about 7:00 AM, he'd then unload and get some sleep. That evening, he would load the truck again, departing about 9:00 PM for the overnight run back to Tokyo. After unloading, he would then get a day off. Repetition of this three-day cycle was the standard work pattern.

This system was very demanding on the drivers, so the relay system was a vast improvement. The idea was simple: at Hamamatsu, the midpoint between Tokyo and Osaka, the Osaka- and Tokyo-bound drivers would exchange trailers. In other words, the driver pulling a trailer from Tokyo would wait at an appointed location for the driver coming from Osaka, exchange his trailer for the one the driver coming from Osaka had been pulling, and return to Tokyo with it, while the Osaka driver took the trailer that had come from Tokyo back to Osaka. This let each of the drivers get off work at noon on the second day and go home to rest. The duty-time of the drivers was greatly reduced, resulting in an overall reduction in working hours.

Another move toward increased productivity was the separation of the tasks of driving and loading. Standard practice among trucking companies was to assign two men to each truck—two drivers on long-distance routes, or a driver and a loader on local routes. Why? Because they were intended to do both driving and freight handling.

It seemed to me that separating these functions was essential to rationalizing our operations, and I decided to be thorough about it. A truck has only one steering wheel, so having two drivers made no sense, and merely added to our labor costs. Off the truck, personnel could be engaged in other work, or in taking rest-time, but once aboard the truck, even if all they were doing was sitting in the passenger seat, it counted as duty-time, and had to be paid for accordingly.

So I reduced the number of on-board personnel to a single driver, and had the freight handling taken care of by on-site personnel specialized in that task. The problem then became one of how to increase the efficiency of these freight-handling operations.

In truck transport, loading and unloading of freight eats up a lot of time. Streamlining this process was one of the keys to raising productivity. From experience I knew that it took about 15 minutes to load or unload a ton of freight—and thus about 150 minutes, or two and a half hours, to handle the load of a ten-ton truck.

So how could this freight handling be speeded up? There was a way: the unit-load system. What this meant was that items would not be handled individually, but grouped into larger fixed-size loads, and handled as such at each stage of the game—from storage and shipment to loading and unloading. New hardware was required to make this possible.

Palletization, for example. A pallet is a low platform of latticed wood on which packages are grouped so that they may be stored and moved as a unit, using a forklift. This system is used in almost every factory in Japan. Then there is containerization, by which much larger loads are consolidated into standardized containers, a system used for almost all maritime and railroad freight shipping.

So what sort of unit-load system could be devised for truck freight? Well, the trailer of a tractor-trailer rig could be seen as a container on wheels. However, as I just mentioned, loading one of these ten-ton containers with individual packages can take two and a half hours. In fact, it was when Yamato introduced these large trailers that we first noticed what an enormous cost we were incurring in terms of loading time. If we continued to load packages individually, there was no way we were going to see the kind of leap in labor productivity I had hoped for when I decided to introduce the tractor-trailer system.

There had to be a way to make this process more efficient. The solution I hit upon was the roll-box pallet: a boxlike pallet on wheels that became our standard unit for storage, freight handling, and shipping.

At first glance, this system seemed to have a drawback in terms of inefficient use of space: the space lost above, below, and between the roll-boxes when they were loaded into the trailers. Because of this, space utilization per trailer fell to about 70 percent of full capacity. In the trucking business the normal tendency is to push the capacity of the trucks to the limit in order to maximize shipments, as you might guess from the fact that overloading is frequently a problem. But I was determined to go ahead with the roll-box pallet system anyway, because my priority was on increasing labor productivity, not freight capacity.

From the standpoint of freight capacity the system was certainly inefficient, even wasteful. But sixteen roll-box pallets could be loaded into the trailers in two parallel rows of eight pallets—with a total loading time of only five minutes! Cutting two and a half hours down to five minutes, with the tremendous savings in labor costs this entailed, more than made up for the 30 percent drop in loading capacity.

I made the decision to introduce the roll-box pallet system in 1971. Two years later, in 1973, it was launched at our Utsunomiya branch, and gradually implemented throughout our operations. We currently use more than 4 million roll-box pallets.

The Difference Between Managing Secondary and Tertiary Industries

From the mid-1950s to the mid-1960s I learned from seminars a number of quite useful ideas regarding labor productivity that I then applied to my management of Yamato. But I was not done learning—I continued to work at absorbing new managerial theory.

My next big lesson was the difference between managing secondary and tertiary industries. It came at a lecture at the Tokyo Chamber of Commerce and Industry (TCCI).

In 1973 I became an officer of TCCI, and was appointed vice-chairman of its Transportation division and a member of various committees.

In addition to its other work, TCCI sponsors a variety of lectures and seminars. Beginning in the mid-1960s, Japan's wave of rapid economic growth had spurred talk of a "distribution revolution" and a push to modernize both the wholesale and retail sectors of the economy. In manufacturing (secondary industry), modernization of management was proceeding apace, with a shortening of working hours and introduction of a five-day workweek, but in tertiary industries such as commerce and transportation the pace of change was much slower. At TCCI we had numerous meetings, centered in the Commerce division, advocating shorter working hours.

On the day in question, I was attending a lecture given by a young researcher from an organization affiliated with the Ministry of International Trade and Industry. Suddenly I heard him saying, "Tertiary industry such as commerce is often seen as not being modern because in comparison with manufacturing the scale of the enterprises is smaller and work hours are longer—but don't let this bother you; this is inherent to this type of industry, and cannot be avoided."

Startled, I pricked up my ears.

> The market sphere of manufacturing is extensive: many products are nationwide brands, and even local brands are marketed to regional blocs. Compared to this, the market sphere for retail sales is quite narrow. Even for large department stores and supermarkets it is limited to the city in which they are located, and often to a radius of a few kilometers. But perhaps the most radical difference between the two is that while manufacturing companies hold inventory and can take their time selling it, for retailers it is a day-to-day struggle. Especially in businesses like hotels and transportation, there is no 'inventory' to hold. Today's leftover rooms or seats cannot be sold tomorrow. Because of this, it is natural for retailers to develop and operate a large number of small-scale outlets. Moreover, in order to reduce the possibility of missing a potential sale, they have no choice but to have extended hours of business. It is a mistake to try to meet this need by extending the working hours of employees. But it is an even bigger mistake to assume that for tertiary industries, modernization means a five-day week and an eight-hour day.

Hearing this, the scales fell from my eyes. The seminars I had attended up to this time were all oriented toward management of secondary industries, drawing their cases from American corporate management. I had learned a lot from this, and put a fair amount of it into practice, but had always had a sense that something didn't quite fit.

On the other hand, it was not as if I had never heard commerce discussed in a seminar—especially when, in the late 1950s and into the 1960s, supermarkets drew a great deal of attention as the standard-bearers of the distribution revolution. I was also deeply influenced and stimulated by the arguments set forth in a book on distribution by Hayashi Shūji, an assistant professor at Tokyo University, which was much discussed at the time.* If I may summarize, Professor Hayashi's theory went something like this:

---

* Hayashi Shūji, *Ryūtsu Kakumei* [The Distribution Revolution], (Tokyo: Chuokoron-sha, 1962).

In the late 1950s the manufacturing sector began to make great progress in the rationalization of production, and production costs fell sharply. But retail prices did not fall accordingly, because of the high cost of distribution after the products left the factories. There were several overlapping layers of wholesalers before one got to the retailers, the majority of whom were small, family-owned enterprises. In order to support cheap mass production you must have mass consumption, which in turn requires mass distribution. Modernization of the distribution system is essential to achieving this. Specifically, shifting from a dependency on small-scale retailers to big mass-merchandise outlets. Shortening the distribution route from manufacturer to retailer by streamlining the redundant layers of wholesalers separating them. Developing entirely new distribution channels, such as selling cosmetics and underclothes at public baths.

In other words, the key to modernization is making distribution channels as broad, direct, and numerous as possible. I agreed completely with this analysis.

Let's return for a moment to the present.

Right now, the retail industry is engaged in more intense competition than ever before. As a result of deregulation, department stores are no longer required by the Large-Scale Retail Stores Law to restrict their hours of operation from 10:00 AM to 6:00 PM and close one day each week. It has now become standard to close only one day a month and to stay open until 8:00 PM.

Moreover, it is now common for famous department stores like those in the Ginza district to have hundreds of branches nationwide. Most of these are not stand-alone stores, but units in larger shopping centers, but the trend has definitely been toward an increasing number of outlets. This means that the individual outlets have to be small-scale, which in turn means that they must maintain a broad but shallow inventory. In other words, they must work to keep their in-store stock to a minimum while at the same time displaying a full product line—two conflicting missions that must somehow be reconciled. How is this to be done? The answer is a distribution system that makes it possible—on a nationwide scale—to frequently restock a large range of products in small quantities.

The same is true in the transport trade. The times demand that we free ourselves from thinking based on the large-scale, large-volume operations of secondary industry and provide new services conceived in terms of tertiary industry.

The Transformation of Logistics

This will take us away from the main theme of this chapter, but I'd like to continue the discussion of distribution begun in the last section.

As we have seen, cutting distribution costs is essential to a company's success in the face of intense market competition. Since a major portion of distribution costs is taken up by logistics, it is only natural that the distribution revolution of the 1960s demanded a transformation of logistics as well. So what is logistics?

The main elements involved are transport, storage, handling, packing, processing, and information. Among these, transport is unavoidable insofar as the sites of production and consumption are separated from each other. Efforts to reduce transport costs—through high-volume shipping, shortening of shipping routes, development of new transportation systems, etc.—are urgently required. By new transportation systems I mean door-to-door shipping, integrating cheap long-haul transport by rail and ferry with local trucking directly serving clients at either end—all accomplished without cargo reloading. Container systems are a concrete example of this kind of integrated shipping.

Storage is much the same story as transport, in that it is an absolutely essential element as long as the sites of production and consumption are separated by any distance. However, the function of warehousing has shifted from long-term storage of raw materials and finished goods toward product distribution centers that provide a means of inventory control.

In any case, transport and storage are absolutely essential elements of logistics. But handling and packaging are different. They have existed as necessary evils, but it would be preferable to dispense with them.

Freight handling can be virtually eliminated by palletization and containerization, which will also make packing (to protect individual items from contact with one another during shipping and handling) increasingly unnecessary.

In terms of logistics, "processing" means the sorting, arranging, and sizing of goods in accordance with shipping orders. "Information" is essentially concerned with inventory management. Both of these elements were originally aspects of distribution proper, but the more they are integrated into logistics, the greater benefit there is from rationalization.

Transport, storage, handling, packing, processing, and information—what is needed to revolutionize the work of logistics comprised of these disparate elements is the concept of systematization. For instance, when a company is building a distribution center, it should unify and systematize the logistical functions of storage, processing, and information. Only by such systematization can distribution costs be reduced.

Here is a concrete example. I will never forget my amazement when, in 1967, the U.S. shipping firm Matson Navigation Company, Inc., introduced container ships on its trans-Pacific routes. Up to that time, export freight had been hauled by truck from factories to the harbor, where it was stored in warehouses. When a freighter docked, its hold would then be loaded by longshoremen employed by a harbor freight-handling company. After crossing the Pacific to America, the reverse of the process would take place—the freight, off-loaded by hand, would be stored in a warehouse awaiting the shipper's order to truck it to its final destination.

The advent of container ships changed all this. First of all, the harbor itself was transformed. The warehouses disappeared from the wharfs, replaced by extensive open yards where containers could be stacked. Export freight was now loaded onto containers at the factory. The containers were then loaded onto trucks using a "hook and drop" system, hauled to the harbor, and delivered to the yards. When the container ship docked, the containers were transferred to the ship and stacked on deck by immense cranes. With the introduction of containers, the majority of dock workers disappeared—yet loading that once took a week or ten days could be completed in a single day, with the ship ready for immediate departure.

The revolutionary aspect of these aluminum containers is that after loading at the factory, they are handled as units. The container serves as the cargo trailer on a tractor-trailer rig for transportation on highways; reaching the port, it takes the place of a warehouse; loaded onto the ship, it substitutes for the cargo hold. From producer to purchaser, the only time the freight leaves the container is when it is unloaded at its final destination. Because of this, packing becomes unnecessary, and damage to goods eliminated. Seeing this container system in use for maritime transport, I keenly felt the power of systematization.

At present, container-based transport systems are being used for domestic as well as international freight. JR Freight (Japan Freight Railway

Company) has implemented containerized freight services throughout the country under the name Freightliner. At first this did not offer the full advantage of containerization, since the containers were created by subdividing old Japan National Railways freight cars, producing containers of an unusual size, incompatible with direct loading unto trucks. However, when JR Freight converted to containers matching the international standard of twenty feet in length, this service found widespread acceptance.

Matson began running its container ships in the autumn of 1967. The following autumn Japan's NYK Line put its first container ship, the *Hakone Maru*, into service, and Japan National Railways ran its first Freightliner in the spring of 1969. The age of containerization had suddenly arrived. The transformation of logistics had finally begun in Japan. But compared to the revolution in distribution, it was off to a late start, and the pace of progress was slow.

OTHER LESSONS: MARKETING, TYPES OF OPERATION, PARTICIPATORY MANAGEMENT

Before ending this chapter I would like to touch briefly on a few other lectures that had a real impact on me—though these came after I had launched our Takkyūbin operations.

With the transformation of logistics, the waves of modernization finally began to reach the shipping industry. But within the trucking industry itself there was virtually no awareness of the need to change with the times.

This spurred me to create the National Council of Transport Enterprises in 1972, with the idea of giving young executives in the trucking industry a forum in which they could seek out new ideas and information and learn new managerial techniques. In addition to publishing a monthly newsletter, the Council sponsored an annual Management Conference for its members, selecting a theme for each year and inviting well-known authorities in that field to give lectures and lead discussion. Three of these lectures had a lasting impact on my philosophy of management.

The first was by Nakata Shin'ya, senior researcher at the Distribution System Research Institute (now a professor at Kanagawa University), given at the sixth annual Management Conference, held in the city of Toba in Mie Prefecture in 1976. His talk, "Methods and Practice of Logistics Marketing," really opened my eyes to the concept of marketing.

Up to that point I'd never heard the words "market" or "marketing" applied to the transport industry. In the industry, the emphasis was solely on service to the client, whom it was common to treat with almost feudal deference.

Executives would often speak of fierce competition in the industry, but all their energies went into holding on to regular clients in a limited region. There was no thought of developing new clients—much less any concept of the market.

So why did we invite Mr. Nakata to speak at the conference?

Not long before, textile wholesalers in Tokyo's Nihombashi district had restructured their delivery system, successfully cutting the freight fees they were paying. For the freight companies, of course, this drop in freight rates was a serious matter. When we looked for the mastermind behind this move, we found that Mr. Nakata was leading the wholesalers' research group. In inviting him to speak, we were trying to pick the brains of one of the members of the "enemy" general staff.

Nakata began by saying that it was now simply common sense to base sales activity in the transport industry on the market. He then expanded upon this theme.

> Marketing is done in order to discover what the consumer wants, and this information is used in product development and merchandizing. Since marketing is the core of sales activity, to an outside observer it seems awfully strange that people in the transport industry are not thinking about it.

At the time trucking companies took their dispatch scheduling and labor management quite seriously, but sales efforts amounted to little more than making the rounds of the established clients. Not only was there no thought of the market—virtually no one had even heard the word "marketing." In this respect, Yamato Transport was no different from the rest, so when Nakata spoke of the market, his words were etched in my mind.

A lecture by Miyashita Masafusa, executive director of the Distribution Policy Institute Co., Ltd., taught me the concept of "type of operation." His talk, given at the eleventh annual conference held in Nagano in 1981, was entitled "The Changing Distribution Industry," and the gist of it was this:

> In the postwar era, the distribution industry has seen the rise of many new enterprises, such as supermarkets, that have contributed to its impressive growth. As a result, there is such a diverse range of firms operating in this area that the word "retail" can scarcely encompass them all, and the situation changes every year.

The key word here is "type of operation." We can no longer discuss
the distribution industry without using this concept.

I'd never heard this term before. Up to this time I hadn't been conscious
of the convenience stores that were suddenly popping up all over Japan as
anything more than small-scale supermarkets. Here I learned that they
were a completely different type of operation.

The era had already passed when the supermarkets—large-scale volume merchandisers—were the standard-bearers of the distribution revolution. The new player getting all the attention was the convenience store.
Their market area was tiny; basically the immediate neighborhood. The
stores themselves were small, less than a thousand square feet in most
cases. There were a lot of them, four or five thousand nationwide. They
were open twenty-four hours a day. They carried everything needed in
the home, and the shelves were restocked several times a day, so that no
product would be unavailable. The convenience store system was a kind of
miracle of using the fundamental nature of retail sales to respond to the
needs of the consumer.

The selling point of the supermarkets was low prices; convenience
stores, as the name suggests, sold convenience. And, as I learned, these
different types of operation required different managerial approaches.

Finally, let me touch on the lecture by Professor Shinoda Yūjirō of Sophia
University's Socio-Economic Institute (now the Institute of Comparative
Culture), where I learned the concept of "participatory management."
This lecture, given at the seventh Management Conference in Kusatsu in
Gumma Prefecture in 1977, was entitled "Employee Participation in the
Management of Transport Enterprises."

I had heard Professor Shinoda speak at the Tokyo Chamber of Commerce and Industry a few years before this, and was so impressed by the
uniqueness of his presentation that I invited him to speak at one of our
conferences. Professor Shinoda had studied abroad in Germany, and the
fruits of his research there and his experience in applying them to Japanese
management led him to advocate what he called "managerial partnership."

"Managerial partnership" implies that management and labor
cooperate equally in contributing their energies to the activities
of the company, the fruits of which are then shared by both. It is
different, however, from what is called "worker participation in

management" in West Germany. In managerial partnership, the central attitude is one of sharing knowledge and sharing work. One of its characteristics is that it encourages greater initiative and self-regulation on the part of the employees. Because of this, it is essential to share necessary information on the managerial environment, personnel issues, and so forth with the employees, so that they are oriented to sharing the goals of management. To encourage initiative on the part of employees, reform of internal communications, small-group work, and a share in the company's success are crucial. How this sharing is to be implemented is something that should be discussed by all, with the entrepreneur making the final decision. Quality is more important than quantity. . . .

Professor Shinoda placed particular emphasis on the importance of communication. His idea was that if employees were given the same information as the company president, then they would think and respond in similar ways. "Managerial partnership" meant that employees would intuit what the president wanted, and act of their own volition to realize it.

But the difficult part of this internal company communication is that all employees have to be provided simultaneously with the same amount of information—since any employees left out of the loop might resent it, and adopt an uncooperative attitude. Phenomena such as factionalism and political infighting within the company all have their source in inequitable flows of information, according to Professor Shinoda.

In the transport industry, where employees of necessity spend much of their working hours away from the direct supervision of their superiors, it would be a real blessing if they were independently and willingly working to achieve the goals of management. I was quite intrigued by the prospect of managerial partnership making this possible, and I immediately set about the creation of a participatory management system at Yamato Transport. I will relate this process in detail in chapter 9.

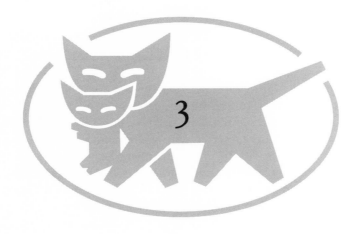

Shifting Markets

I n this chapter I will talk about the factors that led (or perhaps forced is a better word) Yamato Transport into its experiment with Takkyūbin: the dead end our diversification strategy had run into, and the subsequent shift in our target market from commercial freight to home parcel delivery services.

After the war, when Yamato Transport had been too slow in getting into the long-distance freight market, the answer seemed to be diversification, and the creation of a distribution conglomerate. Forwarding operations, department store deliveries, air and maritime shipping, packing services—we would do it all. Yet even as one after another of these enterprises ran aground, our problems were blamed on having focused too exclusively on pursuing major freight clients, and even the profits on our core business of commercial freight trucking began to decline.

Yamato was in trouble, and as the newly appointed president of the company, what came to my mind was literally a vision of reversing the company's fortunes. Maybe it was time to shift our target from commercial freight to home delivery, and abandon our diversification strategy for an opposite tack—focusing all our efforts on a single service.

The inspiration for this radical change in thinking was Yoshinoya's bowl of beef over rice.

Toward Diversification: Freight Forwarding and Department Store Deliveries

Immediately after World War II, Yamato Transport revived its chartered trucking operations and its freight lines. Supported by the postwar recovery of demand, the company enjoyed steady growth. By 1949, the network of commercial trucking lines we had built up throughout the Kanto region prior to the war was almost completely rebuilt. The outbreak of the Korean War in 1950 created an unexpected boom for Japanese industry, which worked overtime to meet the military procurement needs of the Allied forces, and the increased volume of shipping that resulted boosted Yamato's profits.

In the prewar era, Yamato Transport was exclusively a trucking company, and one that had focused its operations on short-haul freight. But after the war, managerial strategy shifted in the direction of diversifying our enterprise.

The first move in this direction was the inauguration of freight forwarding operations in Tokyo in 1950. Freight forwarding was conducted under license to JNR (Japan National Railways), and mostly involved long-distance freight. Receipt of the license to operate as a forwarder at Shiodome station, the terminus of the Tokaidō Line, was a major business coup for Yamato, which had not previously possessed such a license and had concentrated its business on short-haul trucking. By 1955 Yamato's forwarding operations were accounting for 21 percent of the company's total revenue.

Another pillar of Yamato's operations was as a subcontractor for department store deliveries. Before the war Yamato subcontracted all of Mitsukoshi's deliveries. The intensification of the war brought an end to this arrangement, but it was revived in December 1949. In 1954, when the Daimaru department stores began to penetrate the Tokyo market, Yamato also subcontracted their deliveries. This was followed by similar arrangements with Isetan, Sogo, and Takashimaya, so that Yamato came to hold a lion's share of the market for department store deliveries in the Kantō region. By 1959 department store deliveries accounted for another 21 percent of company revenues.

Nor was this the end of Yamato's policy of diversification. From 1950 to 1955, beginning with the securing of a customs license, Yamato expanded into air and maritime freight, harbor transport, packaging, and the like. These newly developed enterprises accounted for 23 percent of total revenues by 1955.

As a result of all this, trucking—once the sole source of revenue—now accounted for less than half of Yamato's total corporate revenues. The goal of diversification seemed to have been reached.

Declining Performance

With diversification, initial results were good: revenues grew steadily, and in 1960 the company posted a pretax profit ratio of 3.1 percent.

On the other hand, a major problem had arisen. Yamato's core trucking business was going into a gradual decline.

Ideally diversification starts from a dependably profitable core business, to which profits from subsidiary enterprises are added. But in Yamato's case, a faltering core business was being propped up by the creation of new enterprises. This was not without value, of course—but the fact that the new enterprises were not growing fast enough to offset the decline of the core trucking business was something that cast a shadow over the future of the company.

Then, around 1970, the company's performance fell off sharply. The diversification strategy itself was running aground. The following year I gave up my post as executive director to replace my ailing father Yasuomi as president of the company.

The first signs of trouble were in the freight forwarding division. The reason was the declining fortunes of JNR.

In 1959 JNR made a policy decision to convert to exclusive use of five-ton containers and launched a high-speed, nonstop container train on the Tokyo–Osaka route that proved to be a hit. Thanks to this, the profits of Yamato's forwarding division also rose sharply.

However, JNR was plagued by incompetent managerial strategy and deteriorating labor relations, and the volume of freight it handled soon leveled off. The fatal blow was probably the massive "right to strike" strike of January 1975. In 1987 JNR was broken up, privatized, and relaunched as JR. At the end, JNR freight services were bringing in ¥200 billion of income on expenditures of more than ¥400 billion—posting a truly pathetic deficit of ¥200 billion. Conflict between labor and management was the primary cause of the shortfall, but a structural void in JNR operations should not be overlooked as a factor.

JNR took responsibility for the management of its on-rail business, but it left other essential operations, such as liaison with shipping clients and the pickup and delivery of freight, completely to its forwarding agents. The railway stations were JNR facilities, and JNR Freight handled the work proper to it, such as the loading and unloading of freight cars and the coupling of them into trains, but there was an absurd legal situation by which the on-rail operations were regulated by the Railway Operations Law, while operations within the stations were regulated by a completely different law, the Express Business Law.

As a result, JNR itself was unable to select agents essential to its operations—forwarding agents were selected and licensed at the whim of the Ministry of Transport, which left JNR in the position of having to use agents that were not necessarily up to the job.

Moreover, the forwarders chosen in this manner were all trucking companies before receiving their licenses, and there was a built-in conflict of interest. The forwarders would skim off the choicest freight for their company's trucking operations, leaving less desirable lots to be carried by the JNR freight trains. Given this situation, it was small wonder that JNR's performance suffered. At the time, the phrase "10-percent forwarders" was a kind of inside joke in the industry: in other words, the forwarders were making 90 percent of their income off their trucking operations, and only 10 percent off their work for the railroad.

In any case, the decline of JNR hit Yamato Transport hard, and our income from forwarding operations stalled out. Once more than 20 percent of our revenues, by 1975 it had slumped to little more than 10 percent. The forwarding division that had been created to prop up the faltering trucking division was now itself a burden.

The next shadow fell over our department store operations. Department store deliveries had mirrored the growth of the Japanese economy as a whole, expanding rapidly year after year. Yamato's revenues from this trade rose accordingly. Yet ironically, the increasing volume of deliveries was attended by a gradual decline in profits.

Department store deliveries have a distinctly seasonal character, with deliveries during the New Year's and midsummer gift-giving seasons running seven to eight times those of off-season months. We handled ordinary months with our regular staff, but these peak periods required hiring more than five thousand students and other part-time help to assist with the huge volume of deliveries. For many years we would rent empty warehouse space to serve as temporary distribution depots, and lease as many bicycles as we had part-time workers, so they could deliver the goods.

In this mode of business, there were few fixed costs and many variable ones, so the break-even point was low. In ordinary months profits would be low, but this would be offset by the major profits realized in the two peak months of July and December.

However, with the volume of deliveries growing annually, we found ourselves forced to turn some of the temporary depots into permanent facilities, and also to buy a certain number of the bicycles outright. In this manner, our fixed costs also grew, beginning to eat slowly but steadily into profits. Ordinary months began to show a deficit, and the two peak months now had to fill the hole left by the other ten months of the year.

Then, in 1974, came the Oil Shock. Its impact was tremendous. As I have related in the prologue, our largest client, Mitsukoshi, demanded a reduction in our delivery rates and as part of its rationalization efforts closed one of its distribution centers, which it then forced us to lease from them for ¥66 million a year. All of this hurt us, and things reached the point that our Mitsukoshi depot alone was losing more than ¥100 million per annum.

But there was worse yet to come. Soon even our core business of trucking hit the wall. In Yamato's case, since short-haul trucking had been our main strength since before the war, in the postwar period our revenue from freight charges did not keep pace with increases in the total volume of freight. Because of this, we watched and grumbled about our misfortune as our rivals began to make a mint on long-distance trucking lines.

In 1960 Yamato finally initiated long-distance freight service on the Tōkaidō route linking Tokyo and the Kantō region with the Kansai region centered on Osaka and Kyoto. Yet compared with the Kantō region, Yamato Transport was virtually unknown in the Kansai, and all the major shipping clients had established relationships with other firms, so we had a hard time digging up any freight to carry. The nearly ten-year advantage our rivals had on us was depressingly vast, and I will never forget how painful it was to be so far behind the game..

Our trucking division had hoped to use the opening of the Tōkaidō route to pull out of its slump, but the anticipated results were not forthcoming, since a latecomer like Yamato had to rely on large-volume shipments at low rates in order to win freight contracts.

Here I need to explain a bit about basic types of trucking operation. In route trucking, a terminal is established in major cities at either end of the route, with regularly scheduled trucks running between them. As a result, the necessary capital investment is quite large. This is also a type of operation that relies on carrying mixed shipments of small-lot freight, since small-lot freight has a higher profit margin, and you can make more money off of loading your trucks with mixed shipments than you can by chartering them to a single customer for exclusive transport of his cargo.

On the other hand, chartered trucking carrying single large loads does not require the investment in maintaining terminals; it is usually run as a local or regional operation. If you try to do this as a route operation, it won't support the needed capital investment and you have no hope of turning a profit. This is particularly obvious with regard to long-distance routes. We knew this, but we couldn't send trucks back empty from Osaka to Tokyo. So we wound up filling them with discount shipments at rates no better than chartered freight.

The declining revenues of our core business, the trucking division, threatened the very existence of the company. So in August 1970, I set out a five-year plan, beginning that year, to carry us to 1974. Here is the gist of it:

1. Make a concerted effort to widen our operations, based on the concept of an expanding equilibrium
2. Make the most of our character as both a common carrier and a general logistics company
3. Make our fundamental goal providing logistic services that deliver the goods when, where, and in the amount the customer wants, always at a reasonable price

It was a pet theory of mine that to allow a contracting equilibrium to continue would end in negating the very existence of the company. That was why I made an expanding equilibrium the basis of the five-year plan. What I did not realize at the time was that my belief that a successful company should be based on satisfying any and all forms of consumer demand for logistic services was nothing more than an illusion.

The retuning of our operations along the lines of the five-year plan resulted in an annual increase in revenues from our trucking division of about 25 percent, but the Oil Shock of 1973 led to a major drop in both revenues and profits. In 1974 we implemented a number of emergency measures to deal with this sudden fall-off in business. I put a freeze on all new hiring, and also laid off about a thousand of our part-time and temporary workers, going from a workforce of about 6,500 employees in 1973 to about 5,500 in 1975. (The fact that I did not terminate a single union member during this crisis would later make it easier for me to win the trust of the union, and gain its cooperation in the launch of Takkyūbin.)

In any event, the layoffs were strictly an emergency measure. I was acutely aware that more radical measures were needed to deal with the sudden decline in both the trucking and forwarding divisions.

In the early 1970s, out of pride in our status as one of the country's largest trucking firms, I had issued an order calling for expansion of sales in all categories: large shipment, small shipment, long-distance, short-haul—go out and get 'em! But the fact that other companies were making a profit while Yamato was not was not simply a matter of insufficient effort on the part of our sales team; I realized there was a structural problem at the base of it.

As I pointed out in the first chapter, Yamato's shipments tended to be made up of larger numbers of units than those of its competitors. In October 1972, a year after taking office as president of Yamato, I had my planning team draft "A Proposal for Systematizing High-Mix Low-Volume Shipping" and had it distributed throughout the company. But it failed to gain widespread support—perhaps because it represented a 180° turnabout from the company's previous policy of going after large-volume shipments.

A Tale of Two Markets

There are essentially two markets for the transport industry. The first is commercial freight: the transport of goods from the producer to the consumer. A factory produces hundreds or thousands of units a day. After leaving the factory, these goods pass through a complex distribution chain in order to reach the consumer for final sale. In this process they may be handled by a number of different strata of national, regional, and local wholesalers before they wind up on the shelves of a retail outlet. And with each of these transactions, ownership of the goods is transferred and the goods themselves transported to a new location. This is the basis of the market for commercial freight.

But there is another market for transport that has nothing to do with commercial transactions. It might involve country cousins shipping fresh vegetables to their urban relatives, or a husband on a temporary out-of-town work-posting sending his laundry home. This market for transport develops spontaneously out of the demands of people's private lives.

The first market is seen as a necessary component of industrial activity, a primary aspect of the logistics supporting all distribution. Its characteristics are repetition (goods are shipped on a regular schedule), regularity (shipping routes are fixed according to the shipper), and volume (shipping lots are large- or mid-sized)—making it easy for the transporter to deal with. The majority of the trucking business is conducted with this commercial shipping market as its target.

This work is further subdivided into various types of operation, largely differentiated by the type of goods they carry and the type of truck needed to carry them: tank trucks for gasoline and other liquids; gondolas for grain, cement, and other particulate materials; concrete mixers; special trucks for heavy materials such as steel; dump trucks for sand and gravel, and so forth. Ordinary miscellaneous freight is differentiated less by mode of transport than by whether it is shipped by truck-load charter or mixed, less-than-truckload shipment, but in any case it is this field that has the largest number of companies and the most intense competition.

The second, consumer-oriented market is also divided into charter and mixed-lot shipping. The most typical charter is a moving van, and many general trucking companies are active in this field.

In contrast, trucking companies are not involved at all in the field of less-than-truckload shipments, basically because the demand is so difficult to gauge, since it is contingent (when and from which household a shipping order will come is unpredictable) and irregular (the destinations and routes are also undetermined).

Until the mid-1970s the Japanese postal service was the only operator in this home delivery market. Private-sector firms had not entered it because it was clearly unprofitable, and because the Mail Law restricted the handling of the mail to the postal service, with a maximum penalty of three years in prison for violators.

Now, Yamato Transport had always operated in the first market, for commercial freight. Our regular line trucks handled occasional less-than-load shipments, but they were all strictly commercial. Yet in this commercial freight market, Yamato had been beaten by the competition.

In the late 1970s, there were more than four-hundred licensed route trucking companies in Japan. If we class them by their profit margins, Class A companies had a profit margin of over 7 percent; Class B, over 5 percent; Class C, over 2.5 percent; and Class D firms were operating in the red. By these standards, Yamato was a Class C company on an inevitable slide into Class D. It would have been another matter if all of our competitors were also losing money as the result of a recession—but for a company president it is truly unbearable to see competitors making money hand over fist when your own company is in the red. In those days my thoughts were filled night and day with the question of how I could restore the fortunes of our company.

However, Yamato had some serious handicaps compared to other firms. Yamato's headquarters were in Tokyo. With the exception of Nittsu and Seibu Transportation, almost all other route truckers were regionally based: Seino Transportation was headquartered in Ōgaki in Gifu Prefecture, Fukuyama

Transporting in Fukuyama in Hiroshima Prefecture, and Tonami Transportation in Tonami in Toyama Prefecture. With its base in Tokyo and with a strong labor union, Yamato's wage base had to be higher than these other companies—by an average of perhaps ¥5,000 a month per worker. The transport industry is labor intensive and requires many workers, so personnel costs can run as high as 60 percent of total expenditure. With a ¥5,000 per worker handicap, under normal circumstances we did not have much hope of beating our competitors.

Yamato's business environment offered little grounds for optimism. Having lost out in the commercial market, the outlook seemed pretty bleak for a turnaround, no matter how much effort we put into it. In that case, maybe we ought to look for another line of business, and go after a new market.

Once this thought came to me, I could not let go of it.

Discovering the Home Delivery Market

If we were going to change our line of business, what came to mind was the second market—home parcel delivery. With our know-how gained in department store deliveries, this was an area Yamato might be able to break into.

Once upon a time, department store deliveries had been Yamato's cash cow, the principal source of the company's profits. But as I have mentioned earlier, this changed when the peak yearly gift-giving months began to generate delivery orders so far in excess of normal months that the volume of work in the remaining ten months of the year was no longer sufficient to support the fixed capital investment needed to expand our operations to deal with the peak periods.

Because of this, I had been searching for some sort of work to occupy Yamato's department store division during the slack months. The problem was that just about any kind of shipping work got busier during the year-end and midsummer peaks, and there didn't seem to be any type of work that could be limited to the off-peak months. However, it occurred to me that while the department store peaks generated seven or eight times the shipments of normal times, noncommercial shipments by individual consumers probably did not even double in volume between off-peak and peak months. This was worth looking into.

However, when I began to consider concrete proposals along these lines, there seemed to be so many obstacles that I hesitated.

At the time, consumer parcel delivery was completely in the hands of the Japanese postal service. JNR also had a small freight service; but, plagued by its gargantuan accumulated deficits, the railroad company was poised to abandon it to concentrate entirely on containerized freight. The postal service's small parcel service was a de facto monopoly.

This meant that the postal service would be our sole competitor, which made for a pretty desirable market situation. But I also knew it was a market we could not easily enter.

There was a reason why no other private-sector companies were active in this market: profitability. No one thought it would pay off. So parcel delivery came to be regarded as a state monopoly, and one that had supported its operations through a steady series of price hikes in the postwar period.

To my mind, everything has its merits and demerits, and nothing is made up solely of one or the other. Fair weather is nice—but too much of it brings drought. A lot of rain is depressing—but it fills the reservoirs with needed water.

The same could be said of the transport market.

In the market for commercial freight, there is regular demand. Contracts with specific clients yield predictable income. But competition is stiff, so rates are low. And you must resign yourself to being paid long-dated promissory notes. Yet the merit of stability and continuity of operations is a major aspect of this market.

On the other hand, in the home parcel delivery market, demand is great but also completely unpredictable, with orders coming at random from a huge number of individuals. Moreover, the destination of the goods is also unknown until you arrive at the client's house for pickup. You may spend a lot of time searching for their address, and upon arrival find that the single small package you are picking up is bound for one end of the country or the other. All of this incurs costs—and yet you can't expect to charge higher rates than the postal service. Rather than making any money, you seem destined to lose it.

But not all the news is bad. Housewives are not going to try to beat down your rates, and they pay in cash. On balance, though, the demerits of this market certainly appeared to outweigh its merits.

Yet as I contemplated this, I also thought that while Yamato may have slipped into Class C, before the war our Yamato Lines had been a household word throughout the Kantō region, and Yamato Transport could still be proud of the fact that it was widely recognized as Japan's largest trucking company. I had a gut feeling that somehow Yamato could find a way to flourish in the home parcel delivery market.

That feeling was backed up by the following thoughts. Regular-route trucking is a kind of public service for an indeterminate but large number of clients. Yet with rising personnel costs due to union pressure, as well as other factors, Yamato had wound up restricting this service to its larger clients, such as manufacturers of household appliances and consumer electronics. In the process we had abandoned individual consumer shipments as unprofitable. It seemed rather heartless to give up on them simply because we weren't turning a profit. Where was my pride as chief executive of a trucking company? Where was my entrepreneurial spirit? I felt that even a hard-headed businessman must have a little romance in his soul, and be willing to pursue his dreams.

The Yoshinoya Model

I've mentioned Yoshinoya before. When I was mulling over launching the new business of home parcel delivery, it brought to mind an article I had read in the *Nihon Keizai Shimbun* some time before that had featured this chain of *gyūdon* (beef-on-rice) restaurants. The article had to do with how Yoshinoya had cut down a more extensive menu to focus on serving only *gyūdon*.

Now I don't know much about restaurants, but it occurred to me that after the war Sapporo *ramen* had become something of a fad. Before the war, if you said noodles, it generally meant *soba*, Japan's traditional buckwheat noodles. But after the war *ramen* became so popular, especially with young people, that it began to challenge *soba* for noodle dominance—to the point that some *soba* shops even began adding *ramen* to their menus. And it seemed to make sense that restaurants should add new items to their menu as consumer tastes changed.

Yet Yoshinoya took the opposite tack, abandoning the rest of its menu to concentrate on *gyūdon*. I was amazed at the audacity of this idea. But wouldn't anyone who didn't want *gyūdon* go to another restaurant? Was this going to work? As an outsider I had my doubts.

However, by specializing in *gyūdon* Yoshinoya was able to buy good beef in quantity at lower prices, and soon acquired a reputation for being both tasty and inexpensive. With only one item on the menu, the customer got a hot bowl of beef and rice almost immediately after ordering. Since the work could be done by unskilled part-timers instead of professional restaurant workers, labor costs were minimized. As a result of all this, Yoshinoya soon had many customers and an enviable balance sheet.

It seemed to me that a successful trucking company would be one that made its customers happy by delivering anything, in any quantity, at any time, to any place, and do this all at a low cost. And I believed that if we set this as our goal and worked hard to achieve it, we could pull past our competition to become the top company in the field. As I sat mulling over our defeat in the commercial freight market and pondering ways of making a comeback, this article I had read about Yoshinoya suddenly came to mind.

Maybe the idea that we had to be able to deliver anything and everything was a mistake! It sounded good in theory, but in fact, in the real world, could we really hope to be that kind of company? Maybe it would be better, like Yoshinoya, to cut our menu down to a single item, and become a company that concentrated solely on consumer parcel delivery, and did not even attempt to do anything else. Which had more genuine potential—being a generalist, jack-of-all-trades sort of firm, or a specialist that did only one thing, but did it well?

Yoshinoya had pioneered an "all *gyūdon,* all the time" type of operation, and the chain had grown and prospered. Yamato's traditional strength had been in parcel delivery for small enterprises and households. Maybe it was time to take a deep breath, change the market we had been going after, cut down our menu, and develop a new type of operation. Maybe this was the escape route from Yamato's difficulties.

I began to think seriously along these lines sometime in 1974.

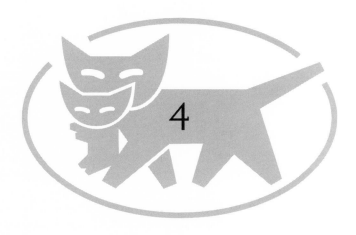

4

Entering the Home Parcel Delivery Market

How were we to storm that citadel of the Japanese postal service, the home parcel delivery market? In this chapter I describe the various hypotheses I came up with in trying to develop and commercialize this unexplored market. You might call it a record of the trial-and-error process that led to the creation of a new type of business: Takkyūbin.

Of course we had rivals other than the postal service, but other transport companies active in commercial freight had stayed away from the home parcel market because of what they saw as its considerable demerits.

A home parcel service could never anticipate when, where, or what sort of packages it would be called on to deliver, so pickup and consolidation of shipments would be terribly inefficient. My work began with questioning this "common sense" assessment, and conversely, thinking of ways in which the process of pickup and consolidation in this market could be made more efficient. My hypothesis was that if we could build a nationwide network to handle this process, we would be on our way.

When I saw four UPS trucks stopped at each of the four corners of a Manhattan intersection, I became even more convinced of the validity of this idea.

Dealing with the Demerits

Why had the home parcel delivery market remained undeveloped? Because people in the transport industry thought it had too many drawbacks.

Commercial freight is shipped on a daily basis from a specific location such as a factory or warehouse, usually to similarly well-established destinations. For example, products of Matsushita Electronics are shipped to Matsushita's retail outlets, Toshiba's to Toshiba outlets, following established routes. Large shipments are the norm; even small shipments do not consist of only a single package. The location of the factory doing the shipping is known in advance; so is the location of the warehouse for which the goods are destined. Given these conditions, all the transport company has to do is deal with the individual clients. If you work in partnership with the client, think of effective ways to improve efficiency, and pay attention to your day-to-day tasks, you are in business.

In contrast, demand for parcel service from individual consumers comes from a different household every time, and the destination could be any inhabited area of the country. As I mentioned earlier, in contrast to the regular and repetitive quality of commercial freight, consumer demand is random and irregular. The home parcel market is one in which you cannot predict the location or volume of demand. And because shipments are virtually all single units, it is terribly inefficient. There would seem to be no way of making this profitable—or so said the conventional wisdom of the industry at that time.

Yet Yamato could not afford to be bound by the limitations of this conventional wisdom. Having failed in the competition for the commercial market, we were trying to figure out how to shift to a new and different market—and nothing would come of it if we gave up because we saw a few drawbacks. The question was how to overcome them.

My role as an entrepreneur was to answer this question. If I could hit upon a method for doing this, and succeeded in implementing it, our only competitor would be the postal service. With no other private-sector firms even in the running, it seemed to me that achieving dominance in this market was no idle fantasy.

The problem was how to gauge demand. So I decided to measure the size of the home parcel market. I sent Yamato employees to about two thousand households in the Chūō 1-chōme and Chūō 2-chōme sections of Nakano Ward in Tokyo, to ask them how many parcels they shipped annually. These neighborhoods were a mixed residential and commercial area fronting Ōme Kaidō, one of the principal routes into the western suburbs from central Tokyo. What the survey found was that on average each household shipped about two parcels a year—almost all of them via the postal service's small parcel service.

My guess was that the actual number was much higher. Why? Because rather than go through all the trouble of wrapping a package and waiting in line at the post office, people were probably buying a lot of their mid-summer and New Year's gifts at department stores, which would handle the wrapping and shipping for them.

At the time, the postal parcel service was handling about 190 million parcels annually and the JNR small parcel service about 60 million, for a total of about 250 million parcels a year carried by existing parcel services. If you figured an average of ¥500 in shipping fees per parcel, this was a ¥125 billion market. Not bad. Certainly large enough to keep Yamato going.

So I knew there was considerable demand for home parcel service. What had me stumped was how to translate this unpredictable and irregular demand into business for Yamato. I simply had no method to deal with the random, dispersed, one-shot nature of the individual orders.

The work of the postal parcel service began when someone brought a parcel to the counter at the post office—a place and procedure everyone was familiar with. But Yamato Transport was certainly not going to get anywhere by asking people to bring their parcels to us. Scarcely anyone would even know where our branch offices were located.

How to collect parcels from individual households—this was a major and unavoidable issue if we wanted to participate in this market. Of course freight collection is one of the fundamentals of the trucking business in any case. With commercial freight the address of the client is a known quantity, so collection is easier. With home parcel service the work only begins with the phone call placing the shipping order—actually getting to the customer's home from the address they give over the phone can take a fair amount of time and effort.

I desperately wanted to turn this into a viable business, but I simply couldn't come up with a plan. As I wrestled with this problem, I suddenly wondered, "Is the demand for home parcel service *really* so random and unpredictable?"

Doubt gave way to a hypothesis. Demand for shipping is born out of the needs of daily life, and even if it seems random when looked at in terms of individuals, in the aggregate it must flow in predictable quantities and directions. If we kept looking at individual demand, we would never find a way to deal with it. But if we were to look at demand in the aggregate, there *must* be a way.

It seemed to me that if you had a bird's-eye view of Nakano Ward, for example, you might see that every day a relatively fixed volume of shipping was leaving it for Osaka, or Sapporo, or Sendai. But how could this actually be measured?

Commercial freight is like taking a gallon jar to the factory, filling it with beans, and carrying it off. Home parcel service is more like a large field over which beans have been scattered—your job begins with having to pick them up, one by one, before you can do anything else.

How? Well, what if instead of sending a ten-ton truck from a central terminal to collect freight from a factory, you had little branch offices in residential areas, with maybe ten minivans that they would send out to do the rounds of the homes and shops in the area, collecting packages?

Commercial freight is like drawing water from a lake. Whether you use a bucket or a pump, it's pretty easy to get it into large drums for shipment. Home parcels are more like underground water. You can't get to it easily from the surface, so how can you draw it? Well, you can drive a pipe into the ground, attach a hose to it, and use a pump to pump it out. Then you put it in drums and ship it.

This kind of thinking led me to the idea of setting up local collection agents. We would ask local businesses used frequently by housewives—the neighborhood saké shop or rice shop, for instance—to serve as agents for us, where parcels could be dropped off. Then our collection trucks could make the rounds of these agents, and consolidate their pickups at a branch office.

Of course the agents would get a per-unit commission—a nice bit of supplementary income for something that didn't involve a lot of effort on their part. And there was benefit to the customer as well. In return for their effort in bringing their parcel to the collection agent, we would charge less than if we had to go to their house to pick it up. And for Yamato, the merit lay in the fact that our parcel collection would be much more efficient. Everybody wins.

When we actually started Takkyūbin operation, saké shops turned out to be particularly enthusiastic about becoming agents for us. There was intense competition among them to secure customers for their stock in trade—alcoholic beverages, soy sauce, and other condiments—and business was not so good. But they soon found that people who stopped by to drop off parcels often bought a bottle of soy sauce or something else as well. On the other hand, rice merchants had a pretty stable clientele in those days, and it seems there was not as much of an advantage to them in becoming agents, since it did little to increase sales.

In recent years convenience stores have enthusiastically joined the ranks of our collection agents, which by 1999 numbered 290,000 nationwide. To put this number in perspective, consider the fact that there are a total of 160,000 post offices in Japan.

The Key: A Pickup and Delivery Network

In order to break into the home parcel delivery market, we would need more than agents collecting packages from individual customers. A nationwide delivery network would also be indispensable.

Personal parcels had to be deliverable anywhere in Japan. This was another point that made this market different from commercial freight. Commercial freight flows according to commercial transactions, and its ultimate destination is a shop located in a commercial district somewhere. This limits the possibilities to something you can deal with. Of course commercial freight will sometimes be sent to an individual consumer, but that is the exception, not the rule.

However, in order to handle personal parcels, which people send to friends and relatives all over the country, you have to build a network that can deliver to any location you are asked to deliver to. Until such a network is in place, you are in no position to take on parcel delivery. So, in concrete terms, what sort of network do you need to build?

There is something known as a "hub and spoke" system. You hear this term a lot in the airline industry. For example, if you want to travel from Japan to a regional city in the United States, you fly first from Narita to the "hub" airport of whatever carrier you have chosen. Depending on the airline it might be Chicago, or Los Angeles, or Dallas. In any case, it will be a major airport to which flights from Japan are bound every day. And from this hub airport, the airline will have connecting flights to cities all over the United States. All you have to do is transfer to the appropriate connecting flight, and you arrive at your final destination quite easily. These connecting flights are collectively known as "spokes," because they radiate outward from the hub airport like the spokes on a bicycle wheel. And so you have the hub-and-spoke system.

A similar system might be considered for home parcel delivery. First you would designate at least one location in each prefecture as the hub for your main-route trucks; in larger population centers such as Tokyo and Osaka, you might have two or three. At Yamato, we call these "bases," and they are linked by daily, regularly scheduled runs by large tractor-trailer trucks.

Serving each base would be twenty or more "centers" from which smaller vans and trucks would be dispatched for deliveries and pickups in the immediate area. These are the spokes. Then, according to need, smaller "depots" used solely for collection might provide support for the centers, supplementing the agents I described earlier.

Customers' parcels would be collected at the depots, consolidated at the centers, and transferred to the bases, where they would be sorted according to destination. After sorting they would be packed into box pallets and loaded onto a large truck bound for the base in the area for which they were destined.

It seemed to me that if we could get this sort of network up and running smoothly, we could deliver anything, anywhere in the country.

The problem was whether or not Yamato was capable of creating the kind of network I had envisioned. Assuming the number of bases to be about one per prefecture, the next thing to figure out was how many of the centers we would need. I came up with the following hypothesis.

The total area of Japan is about 370,000 square kilometers. Discounting uninhabited mountains and wetlands, what would happen if we assembled 1:20,000 scale maps of all populated areas of the country and drew a grid of circles on them, each with a radius of 20 kilometers? Why 20 kilometers? Because our delivery vans averaged about 40 kilometers an hour, which meant that 20 kilometers would be the distance they could travel within 30 minutes of receiving a pickup call. I figured the total number of these 20-kilometer circles would pretty much tell us how many centers we needed.

But when we actually tried doing this, it turned out to be a task of colossal proportions. The way I had formed my hypothesis was at fault. Was there a simpler way? I began to investigate the number of various public facilities.

What about our rival, the postal service? It had about 5,000 collection stations nationwide: a pretty big number. But parcels were only a small part of the postal service's business—ordinary letters made up the bulk of their pickups and deliveries. For parcels alone they shouldn't need so many, so I decided not to worry about this number.

The next thing I tried was the number of public middle schools: 11,250 nationwide. In principle, however, the middle schools were supposed to serve an area within walking distance, so this number was also too large to be helpful.

Finally, I tried police stations: about 1,200 nationwide. This number seemed surprisingly small, but since they were charged with the critical task of preserving law and order in their area, there would have been more if it were necessary. At last, a useful number. If the police could get by with 1,200 stations, Yamato could probably get by with a similar number of parcel centers. So I set our goal at this number.

I had a plan. But was Yamato up to it? First off, we would need money for capital investment. Each base would require a facility of at least 16,500 square meters, and we would have to create at least fifty of them across the country. Could we really survive this financially? Well, worrying never solved anything. We already had a certain number of terminals for handling commercial freight, and I thought we could add to their number gradually. On the other hand, the centers would require between 1,000 and 1,500 square meters each and would have to be created from scratch. The financial burden for this was going to be sizable.

I decided to handle it by leasing all the properties. In terms of ready capital, all this would require was advances on rent and security deposits; after that we'd have to manage somehow.

The issue of an operator's license presented an even greater hurdle. The Road Transportation Law regulating trucking was in force until December 1990, and it stipulated that you could not operate without a license. In December 1990 a new Trucking Business Law would be implemented, shifting to a permission system; but until it went into effect, you could not commence operations without a route-trucking operator's license.

On the eve of commencing our Takkyūbin operations, Yamato Transport's route license was only valid for the Tōhoku region as far as Sendai, the Tokkaidō as far as Osaka, and the San'in as far as Fukuoka. We could not operate north of Sendai or south of Fukuoka; for this, a new license was needed. This was a major pain, but what could we do? Our only option was to make formal application for a new license. The law was eventually reformed and the problem went away, but in the meantime we had an epic struggle with the Ministry of Transport, which I will relate in detail in chapter 8.

When we launched Takkyūbin in 1976, we had 45 bases and 900 centers. In 1997 we were at last able to provide total service throughout the country. Even after that, our network continued to grow; and as of March 1999 we had 70 bases, 1,767 centers, and 238 depots, for a total of 2,715 locations throughout Japan.

The Nature of Network Operations

The biggest question when we were thinking about entering the new market for consumer parcel service was whether or not we could actually make money at it.

Profits were seen as a given in the world of commercial freight, where large-volume shipments were possible, but picking up and delivering single parcels from household to household was a very inefficient sort of work. Everyone thought it was certain to lose money.

I'd hit upon the idea that the work itself could be done if you built a nationwide parcel network, but if the net result was losing money, there wasn't much point to it.

So I began to think about the profitability of network operations. The classic case was telephone service.

In the beginning it was operated by the national government, then became a public utility, and now, after privatization, is known as NTT. Now, of course, we are in the midst of the cell-phone boom, but for quite a while after the war a telephone was not something you found in every household. To get telephone service you had to buy a rather expensive bond and have a utility pole installed, so it was mainly used by businesses. But telephone service gradually began to spread to ordinary households. As a result, the total number of users increased, and the phenomenon of teenagers talking the night away was born. This was also the way in which the telephone became a profitable business.

In its early days, I imagine even the telephone service wavered on the margin between profit and loss. But there is a term, "cross-subsidiary," that describes a situation in which networked operations make possible a kind of internal subsidization, with profitable divisions of a company making up for those that are running in the red.

Home parcel delivery service could be predicated on this kind of "cross-sub" arrangement, with profitability looked at in terms of the network as a whole. The initial costs of building the network would be significant, and with low early use and limited revenue, the system would inevitably start out running in the red. Yet once the network was fully in place, user rates would began to rise, revenues would increase, and you would eventually pass the break-even point and begin making a profit.

It was not necessarily true that you couldn't make money off of home parcel delivery because of its inefficiency. You wouldn't turn a profit until the network passed the break-even point, but as more freight flowed into the network, sooner or later you'd get there. That, in any case, was my conclusion.

But how long would it be before we hit the break-even point? Without knowing that, anxieties remained, and though I was talking a good game about entering this new market, I was in fact not yet ready to take the final step towards making it operational.

The Manhattan Confirmation

It was September 1973. Yamato Transport was involved in international air freight as well, and in April 1971 we opened an office in New York. I had come on a business trip to inspect the office and consult on its operations.

I was also taking in the usual tourist sights. After visiting the observation deck of the Empire State Building for a bird's-eye view of the city, I had just returned to street level. As I stood at an intersection, I suddenly noticed that there was a UPS (United Parcel Service) truck stopped at each of the four corners of the intersection.

UPS is America's largest delivery company. Later, in 1986, it would form a business alliance with Yamato, but at the time I had much to learn from its example as a pioneer in the U.S. trucking industry, and I toured UPS facilities whenever I visited the United States.

When I saw the four UPS trucks stopped at the Manhattan intersection, I had a flash: Profitability of a network was a question of the network as a whole clearing the break-even point—but wasn't there also a break-even point at the level of the individual delivery truck?

The profitability of the network was the sum of the profitability of the individual trucks composing it. And if you looked at the profitability of the trucks, then their daily costs, aside from small variations in mileage, were more or less fixed: labor, fuel, maintenance, depreciation, etc. The question was operational efficiency, i.e., the number of packages the truck could pick up and deliver in a given day. And this operational efficiency would largely be determined by the size of the area the truck had to cover.

The four UPS trucks at the intersection meant that in the heart of the city, trucks were being assigned on a block-by-block basis. What would this translate to in Japan?

Tokyo's Chūō Ward, at the city center, is not that large: approximately ten square kilometers. Yet it would clearly be impossible for a single truck to cover it. If you subdivided it into the districts of Ginza, Kyōbashi, Nihombashi, Tsukiji, and Tsukishima and assigned one truck to each of them, they might manage somehow, but even still, the amount of work they could do in a single day had its limits.

What if you doubled the number of trucks? That would cut in half the area an individual truck had to cover, and double your capacity for pickup and collection. As your operations grew, you might have ten times the number of trucks, with each covering a tenth of the area covered initially by one. If you had fifty delivery trucks in the ten square kilometers of Chūō Ward, each truck would only have to cover two-tenths of a square kilometer. With this small an area, each truck should certainly be able to handle the hundred or so packages a day that it would generate.

It was pretty difficult to figure out where the break-even point for the network as a whole would be, or how many years it would take to reach it, but the per-day costs of maintaining a delivery truck were a known quantity, and the number of packages it needed to handle per day in order to pass the break-even point was also clear. I calculated we would see a profit in something like four or five years.

We could definitely make money in the consumer parcel market. The problem lay in how to increase the number of packages each truck could handle on a daily basis. I knew we had to be able to make money by shifting into this new market—I was totally convinced of it.

But let me digress for a moment. Soon after we had actually started the Takkyūbin service, it was brought to my attention that in some cases our centers, due to a shortage of drivers, were subcontracting pickups and deliveries to small local delivery companies. I absolutely forbid this, for two reasons.

The first was that I believed our drivers should be salesmen as well. If the drivers did not bring in further business with a positive attitude and attentive service to our customers, we would soon be out of business. We might use contract labor behind the lines, but our advance guard, the people with customer contact, had to be company employees—and I put out a strict order to this effect.

Secondly, the profitability of the Takkyūbin service was going to be determined by the efficiency of the delivery trucks. Even if they weren't that efficient in the beginning, and we ran in the red for a while, eventually, if the number of shipments increased, we would turn a profit. But if we were dependent on subcontractors receiving a per-piece payment for each delivery, the profit generated by increasing efficiency would be swallowed by the subcontractor's fees. It took two years of strict enforcement, but I eventually eliminated this type of subcontracting.

In March 1999, the total number of Takkyūbin shipments for Chūō Ward stood at 170,000 for the month: 61,000 pickups and 46,000 deliveries. This volume was divided among nine centers and six depots, using a total of 168 trucks. Each truck handled a daily average of 205 packages. The trucks were all dispatched by the centers; instead of trucks, the employees at the depots use handcarts to make their rounds. The Ginza district has the largest volume of packages in the ward; this small slice of central Tokyo is served every day by 21 trucks, or about 2.6 trucks for each of the district's eight blocks. This certainly beats the four UPS trucks I saw at that intersection in New York those many years ago.

PART TWO

Service Creates the Market

I had set my sights on the consumer parcel market—a plan that the entire management of the company opposed. But Yamato Transport had its back to the wall. I created an action team, invited representatives of the labor union to join, and set it to work developing this new product, thinking as much as possible from the standpoint of the user—the Japanese housewife. If you provide quality service, even if it costs you money, your user base will certainly expand. With "Service first, profits later" as our motto, we launched the Takkyūbin project.

One of the major keys to success was our front-line personnel—the drivers. They were the ones carrying the parcels and directly interfacing with customers. Could they work like forwards in a soccer game, and serve as the key players? My goal was a participatory management style that collapsed the traditional pyramidal organization and inspired and motivated our employees by giving all of them common access to company information. Meanwhile, I pushed ahead with the tasks involved in inventing a new type of operation: constructing a nationwide Takkyūbin network and the information system needed to run it, developing new models of delivery trucks, and so on. We expanded our service lines by adding temperature-controlled "Cool Takkyūbin" and special Takkyūbin deliveries oriented toward ski and golf holidays, and before long our operations were showing explosive growth.

But then we ran up against an unforeseen obstacle. An outmoded regulatory bureaucracy put the brakes on the growth of our network. So I took the Minister of Transport to court. . . .

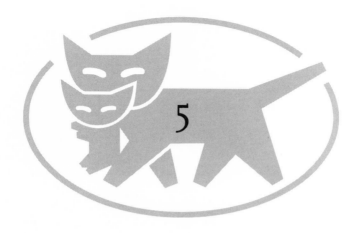

Developing Takkyūbin

What steps did we take in creating Takkyūbin as our weapon in the bid for the consumer parcel market? That is the theme I will address in this chapter.

I was convinced that we could succeed in the challenge of entering this market, and began to plan accordingly, but the officers of the company all initially opposed the idea as being too risky. However, I forged an alliance with the labor union, gradually won over the other executives, and set about making the plan a reality. The key here was that as the top official in the company I had made an executive judgment that this project could be a financial success, and had thought long and hard about what form the operation would have to take in order to succeed. Takkyūbin was the fruit of that effort.

Takkyūbin, which had as its main sales point an easy-to-understand zone system of standard rates and a promise of overnight delivery, was really the first attempt in the trucking industry to market a service as a product.

The hint that proved helpful in conceiving things in this way was Japan Airlines's success in being the first company in Japan to turn the intangible service of "travel" into a branded commodity with the introduction of the "Jalpack."

All Opposed

This new market, aimed at deliveries from individuals to other individuals and thus dependent on use by an unspecified mass of people, had an

advantage in that it would probably be welcomed by the general public—
but it had the disadvantage of being an uncertain financial proposition.

After investigating this disadvantage, and thinking about how to deal
with it, I had concluded that it would not be too difficult to overcome—if
we were not bound by the old ways of thinking prevalent in the trucking
industry, and were willing to come up with a new system for doing business. If we were, I had come to firmly believe that we could readily solve
the issue of profitability, and in fact stood to make a lot of money if we put
in the effort.

So I began to lay the groundwork within the company for introducing
this new enterprise. But the reaction of the other corporate officers was
pessimistic. In their minds was the lesson we had presumably learned
from our department store delivery operations. Once upon a time, the
department stores had been our cash cow, but with rising costs, these
operations gradually slid into the red.

Collection of these deliveries was no sweat—all we had to do was pick
them up at the main stores, which were concentrated in Tokyo's Nihombashi and Shinjuku districts. In contrast, collecting parcels one by one
from households scattered throughout the twenty-three wards of Tokyo
was going to be a nightmare. If we got ourselves involved in that sort of
work we were bound to lose money—or so went the opinion of the rest of
Yamato's management.

My counter-argument went like this:

With department store deliveries, in order to deal with peak period
loads more than ten times those of ordinary months we had to maintain facilities that are excessive for normal periods and increase costs. In contrast,
demand from ordinary consumers will probably do no more than double at
peak periods, so we shouldn't be plagued by unnecessary expenditure on
facilities. Moreover, since department store deliveries are a service keyed
to purchases, if we assume for the moment a purchase price of ¥3,000, the
most that they will bear in terms of a shipping fee is ¥120 to ¥150, while
I believe that for general home parcel service we should be able to charge
around ¥500 per unit.

But the fixed idea that home parcel delivery was horribly inefficient and
could only lead to losses was difficult to dispel—and in the beginning I could
not enlist the support of a single one of the other executives. In company
meetings and every other opportunity I could find, I preached my vision of
the new enterprise, but could not seem to generate any enthusiasm.

But then a voice came from an unexpected quarter: "Well, if the boss is going to keep hammering away at this idea, maybe we ought to give it some serious thought." It was the leaders of the labor union. They were seriously concerned that Yamato Transport was falling into a managerial crisis.

In the normal course of things it should be the company officers, department heads, and other executives that should be giving serious thought to the current position of the company and the issues facing it, and be concerned for its future. But this is not always the case. Salaried managers can be weak on taking personal responsibility and tend to be conformists in thought and behavior. They also have a strong tendency to postpone action, hoping that somehow things will just sort themselves out. On the other hand, labor union leaders are in daily contact with the workers on the shop floor and have a gut sense of how the company is doing. Moreover, through the thrice-annual collective bargaining sessions, they also have a grasp of the corporate balance sheet. So they did me the service of listening seriously to my plan for breaking out of the company's deadlock.

There is a back story to this. In 1973, at the time of the Oil Shock, Yamato had been hit with a sudden and precipitous drop in demand for shipping services, and was forced into a contracting equilibrium. But I promised at that time that absolutely no union members would be laid off, and I kept my promise. The union remained grateful for this effort.

All the executives might still be in opposition, but if the company did not move forward, it would soon feel the pinch. In the April 1975 to March 1976 fiscal year, we had sales of ¥35 billion. But our pretax profits on this were only ¥26.9 million—our profit margin had fallen to 0.07 percent! We could simply not afford wasting any more time trying to convert the unconverted. Yamato was backed into a corner, and action was the only way out.

A Five-Point Plan

To move forward with Takkyūbin, I needed the approval of the board of directors. So I personally wrote up my concept for the new enterprise in a document titled "A Proposal for Development of Takkyūbin," and presented it to the board in August 1975. The basic idea was presented in five points:

1. Our target will be the general public and their parcels.
2. We will think of things from the point of view of the consumer.
3. We will maintain a consistent level of superior service.
4. Our system will be both self-perpetuating and developmental.
5. We will aim for total rationalization of the enterprise.

Let me explain these points in greater detail.

  1. Development of Takkyūbin was predicated on abandoning the commercial freight market in favor of an individual parcel service market rooted in the daily lives of consumers. This premise of focusing on the general public as our target market was a call for a radical change in managerial approach.

  2. Up to this point, trucking companies had normally relied on a roster of regular clients, and had not attempted to target the general public as a market. If we were going to have the general public as our customers, we were going to have to change our way of doing business. From this point on, direct contact between Yamato's sales team and the clients would disappear. In order to understand what this new market demanded, we would have to start thinking about things from the perspective of the consumer. And to do this we would have to adopt the methods of marketing.

  3. In order to break into this new market and win the allegiance of the general public, offering service superior to that of our competitors (at this point mainly the postal service) would be crucial. We could not get by with offering good service only where it was convenient for us—we had to deliver uniformly excellent service to even the most remote areas.

When we were working in the commercial freight market, our clients were the shipping departments of manufacturers and warehouse supervisors. They were well-schooled in the business, knew how long it should take for a shipment to reach a certain destination, and thought it obvious that freight charges should be higher for longer distances. With the general public, and especially housewives, however, we would be dealing with people whose grasp of geography and the distances between cities was not as sophisticated. What we needed to offer them was uniformity: uniformity of both delivery time and delivery cost. Moreover, we could not depend on the customer to have either the skills or the materials to package their goods appropriately. We had to let go of the concepts we had acquired in the commercial freight business, and rethink our services from the ground up.

  4. I spoke of a self-perpetuating, developmental system because I knew the new enterprise would require the construction of a vast network. It could not be done all at once, so my proposal was the gradual creation of a nationwide network.

  5. Takkyūbin was going to be extremely time- and labor-intensive work. Costs would be high, and if we went at things in an ordinary frame of mind we were going to lose money. If we ran in the red with the enterprise that

was supposed to pull Yamato out of its crisis, there wasn't much point to it all. So ingenuity in cost-cutting was absolutely essential. To this end, we had to rationalize our procedures as completely as possible, and especially keep administrative work to a bare minimum.

The plan was approved by the board on the first ballot. Vocal opposition among the top company executives ceased, and they resigned themselves to getting with the program.

Forming a Working Group

As soon as I had received the approval of the board of directors, on September 1, 1975, I set about forming a working group. I picked its ten or so members from among our young executives, and sat in on the discussions in my capacity as company president, along with the executive director for sales and marketing.

One other unique feature of this working group was that I had invited a representative of the labor union to participate.

I'd been impressed by something I'd read at one point in a book by Kaneko Sa'ichirō, who had been a major figure in postwar labor-management policy as the president of Jujo Paper. He stressed the following:

> The thing you have to watch out for in negotiating with the labor unions is giving in to anything that doesn't make sense. Even something that the union is asking for that may appear to have nothing to do with work conditions should not be swallowed unquestioningly—particularly anything to do with money. If you give them a hundred yen, before long that will escalate into a vested interest, and you'll have a tough time getting rid of it again. You always have to watch what you are doing and act consistently.

I agreed with this completely, and had strictly forbidden shop-floor supervisors from negotiating with the union, even on work procedures and other issues that had nothing directly to do with wages and benefits. In other words, I didn't want the union to cut too large a figure in the workplace. After the war, when the union movement was quite strong, my father used to say "Love the workers, but bust the unions." He was a sentimentalist, and took a paternalistic approach to leading the company. Our workers were our employees, but they were also union members. What he tried to do was reduce their consciousness of themselves as union members.

However, on the shop floor various procedural issues come up that really don't involve the conditions of employment. I realized that in such cases it was important for the supervisors to be able to consult with their subordinates. But who should be appointed to represent the opinion of these subordinates? I had gradually come to feel that the logical person for this role was the union shop steward.

As a result, it was natural for me to invite participation by union representatives in the working group I was setting up to launch Takkyūbin. After all, in a company climate of almost total opposition to my idea of shifting from commercial freight to consumer parcel service, it was the union alone that had expressed support, albeit with something less than enthusiasm.

But the union refused to participate. They could see that if they did, they would have to move from passive to active support of the plan. For the most part, labor unions have a habit of opposing anything company management is trying to introduce. They like to demonstrate the union's presence by rejecting any proposal out of hand, and getting the company to propose a compromise. If they participated from the beginning in the working group, they would have to take responsibility for its decisions. So they dragged their feet—though in the end, after a great deal of cajoling, they agreed to join the group.

The kind of people who rise to become union leaders hold clear opinions and are often a bit self-aggrandizing—in other words, if they had followed a slightly different path, they would have made quite capable executives. So I knew what I was doing when I invited them to take part in our corporate meetings. Most Japanese have a strong sense of involvement in their companies, and from that perspective there is nothing to gain and quite a bit to lose by excluding union officials.

At the end of October, after two months of intensive deliberation, the working group drafted a manual for Takkyūbin operations. The contents were as follows:

Marketing Plan for Takkyūbin

1. *Product name: Takkyūbin*
   At first, since we would be specializing in parcel delivery, we thought we would take a page from UPS's book and call ourselves YPS (for Yamato Parcel Service). But in the end, we decided to use the name Takkyūbin. (I'll explain how we came up with this in a moment.)

2. *Type of freight handled*
   We will limit ourselves to individual parcels of ten kilos (25 lbs) or less, with measurements of less than a meter in length, width, or depth. Cardboard boxes or carefully wrapped paper parcels will be accepted.

3. *Service area*
   Incorporated municipalities in the Pacific coastal region of Japan.

4. *Delivery time*
   Generally speaking, overnight delivery; in certain areas, second-day delivery.

5. *Flat-rate service within zones*
   A single fixed rate will be charged for delivery within a zone or the zones surrounding it.

6. *Shipping fees*
   ¥500 per parcel. ¥100 additional for delivery outside the shipper's zone. All fees collectible in cash.

7. *Collection*
   Telephone pickup available even for single parcels.

8. *Agents*
   We will contract with rice shops, saké shops, etc., as collection agents who will display our logo. Customers who bring their parcels to one of these agents will receive a ¥100 discount.

9. *Paperwork*
   A special waybill for Takkyūbin will be created and affixed to each parcel. Standard shipping tags will not be used.

The Watchword is "Freight Density"

The working group had delivered its report in less than two months. However, I had been thinking about the shift from commercial freight to consumer parcels for years now, and had developed fairly concrete notions of how to go about doing it.

If we could establish a nationwide network, we would be in business, though it might take several years before we started making a profit. It was clear that we must be prepared for a number of years of red ink before the new enterprise was really capable of supporting the company and the livelihood of its employees. How many years was anybody's guess, but if we did not make every effort to pass the break-even point as soon as possible, I feared the company might exhaust itself.

Creating the nationwide network of bases, centers, and depots was a massive undertaking, but could be accomplished, given enough time. As the network gradually expanded, the problem would be whether or not we could amass the volume of freight needed to support it.

First comes the all-out effort to create the network. Then freight starts to move through the network on a daily basis. At some point, when it reaches a certain volume, on some days a trickle of profit begins. Eventually those days become greater in number, and from various points in the network these trickles of profit merge into a more dependable flow and begin to accumulate. The exact source of the profit might still be unknown, but the network as a whole would be moving into the black. . . .

This was the image I had in mind, and it seemed to me to represent the nature of a networked operation. The key to whether Takkyūbin would succeed or fail lay in what I began to call the "density" of freight: the volume of freight coming from a specific area. High density meant profits; low density meant losses.

In any case, increasing the volume of freight was an absolute necessity, and once we had started Takkyūbin I stressed the idea "freight density is our watchword" at every opportunity.

But how were we going to increase freight density? By having customers "buy" as much of our Takkyūbin service as possible. Our customers were mainly housewives. What was it we needed to do to get them to buy?

The hint came from another field—the travel industry. In addition to its freight business, Yamato had been operating a chain of travel agents, specifically, agents for the Japan Airlines "Jalpack" tours. Every year the Jalpack head office would convene a seminar for travel agents to introduce the year's new tours and provide other information. When I attended one of these seminars, I was startled to realize that the service of travel could also be turned into a marketable commodity.

After all, travel is a personal thing, and people's destinations and reasons for travelling differ. Once upon a time, if you were planning a trip you would go to a travel agency like JTB (Japan Travel Bureau) and make separate reservations for planes, trains, and hotel accommodations. In those days, travel abroad was largely by businessmen and academics—not casual tourists.

But the postwar era saw the flourishing of the package tour—your flight, hotel, sightseeing tours, meals, and all other amenities included in a single package for a set price. Once you paid your money and got to the airport, everything else would be taken care of by the tour attendants, so that even elderly folks who couldn't speak a word of English could enjoy a holiday in Hawaii. When I attended the Jalpack seminar I learned at first hand how the service of travel was being sold as a commodity.

If this was the case, we ought to be able to find a similar way to get housewives to use our parcel service. What we had to do was make it as easy as possible for them to "buy" our service.

Part of this meant taking the guesswork and anxiety out of the shipping process—reassuring the customers who might be afraid they hadn't wrapped their parcel properly, or who felt they might be taken advantage of in terms of shipping fees but had no way of knowing what was appropriate. A fairly large number of housewives had experiences at the post office that made them reluctant to take parcels anywhere.

In order to put the fears of such customers to rest and have them use our services without hesitation, we had to be very thorough about marketing our services as a commodity. This is the task I had set before the working group, and their answer was the "Marketing Plan for Takkyūbin" whose contents I outlined earlier.

Essentials of the Marketing Plan

Let's take a more detailed look at the key elements of the marketing plan.

1. Product name. Naming is essential to a product—it can determine whether it sells or not. So what should we name it?

Name should express nature, as the saying goes—but what was the essence of our service? Small parcel service for the individual consumer. Simple and convenient, with no need for complicated packing. Speedy, next-day delivery. Inexpensive—about the same as the postal service. What name could express all of this? Unable to think of anything better, our first candidate was YPS (Yamato Parcel Service) following the example of America's UPS. But somehow that didn't have the right ring to it. And *kanji*—the Chinese ideographs used in writing Japanese—seemed to offer a more effective clue as to the content of our services. Wouldn't they be a better choice?

So what came out of this was *takkyūbin*—a newly-minted compound made up of the characters for "home" and "express," plus a third with a rich range of meanings that include "delivery," "post," and "convenience," as well as "regularly scheduled service" (an airline flight, for example). There was some concern that the name might evoke associations with ping-pong (the Japanese word for the game is *takkyū*, written with the *kanji* for "table" and "ball"), but the more we used the word *takkyūbin* in our discussions the better it sounded—the rhythm was pretty good. These days I have many people tell me it's a fine name, and I think we didn't do too badly with it. And of course, it being a product name, we immediately registered it as a trademark.

2. *Type of freight handled*. We decided to limit ourselves to carrying in-dividual parcels of ten kilos or less and with measurements of less than a meter in length, width, or depth, but not without serious debate. The average size for commercial freight is twenty-three kilos (according to a Ministry of Transport study). Because of this, there was strong opinion that we should take packages of up to twenty kilos, thereby increasing the volume of freight we would be handling. But in consideration of the fact that we were going to have to employ women drivers, and that the maxi-mum weight for the postal service's small parcel was six kilos, we settled on a maximum weight of ten.

The reason we insisted on individual parcels was that we wanted to keep the computation of freight charges as simple as possible. Trucking rate schedules were subject to Ministry of Transport approval, and thus could not be set at the whim of the carrier. But these rate schedules were set according to the lot—all parcels going from the same shipper to the same destination—not by the individual parcel. Each lot, no matter how many parcels were in it, would get a single shipping tag, and the weight would be computed as a total for the lot. In order to avoid the complications of this system, we restricted ourselves to carrying individual parcels.

We also decided to be liberal about the packaging we would accept: cardboard boxes were OK, but so were parcels wrapped in paper, as long as they seemed sturdy enough. Rather than reject packages that seemed likely to be damaged because of poor packing, we decided that the Yamato staff accepting the parcels would be responsible for any supplementary packag-ing deemed necessary. This was an important point: if we gave housewives a hard time about the quality of their packing, we would lose their business.

3. *Service area*. Postal small parcel delivery operated nationwide. Obvi-ously, in order to compete with it we had to aim at nationwide coverage, too, but given the realities of our situation and the fact that we were not yet licensed to carry freight in many areas, we had no choice but to limit our service initially to the Pacific coastal region (where the bulk of Japan's

population resides), and within that, to incorporated municipalities. We would then gradually expand into the areas along the Japan Sea, and into unincorporated rural areas.

4. *Delivery time.* Back then, delivery times for postal service small parcels averaged four to five days. If we were to challenge the postal service for control of this market, we would have to do better than that.

Up to that point, conventional wisdom in the industry was to expedite commercial freight, but not to worry much about how fast individual consumer parcels were delivered. I thought this was a mistake.

After all, commercial freight is a result of commercial transactions in which both parties—shipper and receiver—usually build a certain amount of flex into their schedules. In most cases, a day late was not going to be a dollar short.

On the other hand, with private parcels, there was a good likelihood of urgent shipments: things that had to be there for tomorrow's wedding, or tomorrow's flight, or documents that had to be delivered right away. Even if these urgent packages amounted to only one in ten parcels, they had to be delivered overnight. So why not just make overnight delivery standard?

In the case of deliveries from Osaka to Tokyo, a number of shipping companies promised overnight delivery within the twenty-three wards of the city proper. But even municipalities on the outskirts of Tokyo's central wards, such as Fuchū or Koganei, did not necessarily receive overnight service; and when it came to more distant outlying cities and towns such as Ōme and Itsukaichi, most companies offered only second-day service. By the time you got as far away as the town of Okutama, it might take three or four days, and some companies would not deliver to these more remote areas at all. It was easy to promise overnight delivery between Osaka and Kyoto, but considerably more difficult to guarantee overnight delivery throughout the greater Tokyo metropolitan area.

A commercial client might be satisfied if shipments from Osaka arrived overnight to the twenty-three wards of Tokyo and to the major satellite cities close by, such as Mitaka and Musashino, and put up with deliveries to places like Okutama arriving second-day. But housewives would not. If they had relatives in one of the twenty-three wards and in Okutama, they would want packages to arrive at either location the next day, and since Okutama is a popular day trip from central Tokyo for hiking and other activities, it was not as if overnight delivery to it was impossible. In principle, there was no reason it could not be done. But to deliver one or two packages at a time to the distant foothills of Okutama was not economical, and the reason it took packages three or four days to reach there was that shipping companies would consolidate their packages into a couple of shipments a week. It was not that they couldn't do overnight delivery—they were choosing not to.

5. *Flat-rate service within zones.* In selling a product, the most important thing by far is setting the price. Trying to sell cheaper than your rivals is an essential element of competition, but in order for it to work you have to make sure the price is clearly stated, and that your price and product can be readily compared with those of your competitors. If we were going to market Takkyūbin as a product, I believed it was absolutely essential to make the pricing as clear and as simple to understand as possible.

The principle that normally determines commercial freight rates is weight and distance. Computing this is complicated; most shipping companies have clerks specializing in these computations. In addition to being complex, there is another major flaw to this system. Because the fee for each package has to be computed separately, even if you post a rate schedule there is no way to know in advance what any individual package will cost to ship.

With commercial freight this is not really a problem. Commercial freight flows regularly between established clients on well-defined routes, so there is little reason for there to be any dispute between the clients and the freight company regarding the computation of rates.

Parcel delivery for individual consumers is a completely different matter. The reason we set a weight of ten kilos or less as standard was in part to simplify computation of rates. Even so, with different clients and different pickup and delivery points each time, computing the exact distance each piece of freight travels is close to an impossibility. Thus it seemed to me that we had no choice but to introduce flat rates, unrelated to the actual distance traveled.

In businesses catering to the general public, it is very odd not to display prices. At the sushi shop, for instance, people will hesitate to order the items designated "market rate." Freight service is not something most people use every day, so nobody knows the market rate. For precisely that reason, a fee indicated clearly in advance makes it easier for people to use your service without worry.

Thus we settled on a zone system with flat rates within each zone. The issue was how to determine the zones. The larger we made the regions, the simpler the rate schedule would be. For example, the Japanese postal service delivers postcards anywhere in the country for the same rate—the essence of simplicity. But the actual cross-country transport costs for a postcard are minimal compared to the costs involved in parcel delivery, so a single national rate is reasonable. On the other hand, setting a single national rate for Takkyūbin parcels seemed a bit over the top. Our rival the postal service divided the country into five zones for parcel delivery. We had no need to coordinate with them, so we adopted our own zone system for Takkyūbin.

We divided the country into nine zones: Tōhoku, Kantō, Shin'etsu, Hokuriku, Chūbu, Kansai, Chūgoku, Shikoku, and Kyūshū. Delivery to the zone in which the customer resided and to any contiguous zones would be at the same flat rate. For instance, a package from a customer in Tokyo would be delivered at the same rate to the Kantō, Tōhoku, Shin'etsu, Hokuriku, and Chūbu zones. Hokkaidō and Okinawa were treated as special rate areas (and somewhat later we divided the Tōhoku zone into Northern Tōhoku and Southern Tōhoku).

I was surprised, however, at the strength of the opposition that arose within the company to this flat-rate zone scheme. They had trouble accepting the idea that a package going from Tokyo to Yokohama, Shizuoka, or Nagoya should be charged the same ¥500 rate. Or that it should be the same, even within Nagasaki Prefecture, for a package destined for the city of Nagasaki or the more remote Gotō Peninsula. And the manager of our Hiroshima branch office complained—in fact, almost threatened—that if all of Hiroshima Prefecture were figured at the same rate, what with all the people scattered through the islands of the Inland Sea that were part of the prefecture, his office was going to run in the red.

It is true that as distance increases, costs rise, and that delivery to remote mountain areas and isolated islands is particularly expensive. But at the same time, if you factor in the savings in administrative costs resulting from a zoned rate system, it was far from irrational. That was what I said in an effort to convince the doubters in the company. And even more important was the boost to sales that would come about if housewives found the system simple and reassuring and became repeat customers. I explained things in this manner over and over again, and finally won acceptance for the idea that a fixed-rate zone system was not a mistake.

6. *Shipping fees.* Freight rates were still regulated by the Road Transportation Law, and since Takkyūbin was still a type of trucking operation, we had to observe the rate schedule approved by the Ministry of Transport for LTL (less-than-truck load) carriers. According to it, rates should go up with every twenty or thirty kilometers of distance, and a zoned flat-rate system was clearly against the regulations. Yet this was not a fixed rate system; it was a sliding scale in which rates could vary as much as 10 percent above or below the Ministry of Transport benchmarks.

In the approved rate schedule, a ten-kilogram parcel would cost ¥450 if it were sent 160 kilometers, ¥500 for up to 410 kilometers, ¥552 for up to 700 kilometers, and ¥598 for up to 950 kilometers. I was delighted to find that by utilizing the flexible rate system, we could set a flat rate of ¥500 for our intermediate zones and ¥600 for the more distant zones, without violating the letter of the law.

7. *Collection.* As far as collection was concerned, our principle was that we would pick up one or more parcels from any household on request. In contrast to the postal service, which offered no parcel collection service whatsoever, this would allow us to make the most of our higher level of service, and feature it prominently in our advertising.

8. *Agents.* In point of fact, collection was going to be costly both in terms of time and effort, so we decided to establish agents in shopping areas and the like to assist us in receiving parcels. Our goal was to have an agent within a hundred meters walking distance of every household, and we sent out teams to canvass for participating merchants. The agents would receive a ¥100 handling fee for every package they received; the customers would receive a ¥100 discount for bringing their packages to an agent. In other words, for parcels coming to us through the agents, Yamato Transport would receive only ¥300 of the ¥500 shipping fee.

For the customer, having us come to pick up the parcel was easier, but rather than waiting for our van without knowing precisely when it would come, they could take their parcel around the corner when they went shopping, give it to a friendly merchant, and get a ¥100 discount. The merchants would also be happy to get their ¥100 fee, and would cheerfully receive the packages for us. To make this work we really needed agents located within a hundred meters of every home. At present we have about 300,000 agents nationwide, and since the handling fees we pay are a fixed ¥100 per parcel collected, the more agents we have the better.

Thinking of the ¥200 going to the customer and the agent in this way as a marketing cost, I was convinced that it really wasn't too high.

9. *Paperwork.* Bills of lading for commercial freight are not issued for the individual parcel, but by the lot, no matter how many packages may be in it. As a result, what we call broken shipments happen fairly often. This is when certain of the packages in a large lot get separated from the others in shipping, and there is a discrepancy between the number of parcels listed on the bill of lading and the number that have actually arrived. Since the bills of lading and the freight they reference travel separate routes, every company struggles with control of the process.

The reason we decided to limit Takkyūbin to individual parcels was to streamline process management, protect against mishandling of freight, and at the same time to cut administrative costs. To this end, we created special waybills that would be affixed to each parcel and travel with it.

Affixing the waybill to the parcel in this manner is quite dangerous in the sense that there is no way to trace a parcel that is lost in transit, but it simplifies work procedures and achieves a sizable reduction in costs. To help prevent loss of parcels, the waybill numbers can be separately recorded in a computer database.

Open for Business

On January 20, 1976, the organizational and staffing orders were given establishing Takkyūbin service in our Kantō office, and on January 23 it commenced operations. The first shipment was a total of eleven parcels.

Working from our existing field offices, we rolled out our operations to new regions as soon as we had developed the necessary infrastructure.

1976

February

The twenty-three wards of Tokyo and surrounding suburbs, plus urban areas in the six other prefectures of the Kantō region

March/April

The cities of Shizuoka, Hamamatsu, and Sendai

May/June

Major urban areas in Osaka, Kyoto, Aichi, Hyōgo, Shizuoka, Mie, Miyagi, Fukushima, and Fukuoka prefectures

September/October

Major urban areas in Okayama, Hiroshima, Saga, and Nagasaki prefectures; Sapporo and other urban areas in Hokkaidō

1977

Urban areas in Shiga, Tokushima, Kagawa, Oita, and Wakayama prefectures

All locations within greater Tokyo (except for the Izu and Ogasawara islands) and the six other Kantō prefectures

1978

Major urban areas in Yamagata, Nara, Fukui, and Tottori prefectures

All locations in Shizuoka, Nagasaki, Miyagi, Fukushima, and Osaka prefectures (except for outlying islands)

1979
Urban areas in Niigata, Gifu, Ehime, Kōchi, Miyazaki, Yamaguchi, and Toyama prefectures
All locations in Aichi Prefecture; the cities of Kumamoto and Morioka

As a result, at the end of the 1979 fiscal year (March 31, 1980) the physical area covered by our Takkyūbin operations amounted to only 27.4 percent of Japan's total land area, but served 74.8 percent of its population.

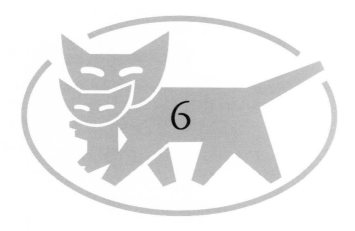

Differentiation of Service

With intangible products such as Takkyūbin, the most important thing in establishing a decisive difference between you and your rivals is what is known as "differentiation of service." In this chapter I will talk about the strategy Yamato employed to achieve this differentiation of service, how it became the springboard for the formation of an entirely new market, and how it propelled the growth of Takkyūbin into a hugely successful product.

What were the services we needed to differentiate with Takkyūbin? Consumers' primary demand with regard to freight is speed of delivery. So Yamato proclaimed "overnight delivery" as its selling point and the principal weapon in its challenge to the postal service monopoly on small parcel delivery. And we set about building a national collection and delivery network that would eventually make this service standard for any location in Japan.

But as I have said, service is an intangible. So you have to have some way of checking whether your efforts at differentiation are working. At Yamato we tracked a large number of individual parcels to get hard data on the success rate of overnight delivery, and found that in many cases no one was at home to receive the parcel when it was delivered. So we developed an "at home" delivery system that was decisive in differentiating our services from those of our rival, the postal service.

Implementing Overnight Delivery
With a feeling akin to leaping off a cliff, we commenced Takkyūbin operations on January 23, 1976. It was a decision backed by considerable thought

and deliberation, but there was anxiety nonetheless. Logically, I believed that this new business was destined to pay off, but it was also a certainty that we would have to get through some rough times before it did.

The key word in attaining profitability was "density of freight." If we achieved it, we would definitely make money. But how? Differentiation of service was the only way. We had to provide better service than the postal service—in concrete terms, overnight delivery. The only way to get the general public to know and use Takkyūbin was to deliver packages overnight, delight the customers, and win their repeat business.

And in fact, the first people to use Takkyūbin were amazed when the parcels really did get there overnight. Customers in Osaka would send a package to Tokyo, still assuming it would take two or three days to get there, and when they called the next day to tell their relatives or friends that the package had been sent, they would be startled to find that it had already arrived! The recipients of the package would also be pleasantly surprised, and would decide to try Takkyūbin the next time they sent a parcel themselves. This was the beginning of great word-of-mouth advertising.

For any freight company, it was a given that TV sets shipped from an Osaka factory would be delivered at a sales outlet in Tokyo the following day. This was because it was a matter of loading the TVs at a factory in Osaka and transporting them to a warehouse in Tokyo. But picking up a small parcel from a private household in Tennōji Ward in Osaka and delivering it to relatives in Tokyo's Suginami Ward was a completely different task.

In freight shipping, the highest value is speed. Reliability and low cost are also important, but speed is the main thing. However, speed alone is not an adequate selling point. Unless you make it tangible, unless you promise "overnight service," it has little impact.

Postal service small parcels would arrive in a couple of days at the fastest, and might take as long as three or four. So Takkyūbin's overnight service was a refreshing change for the consumer, and created good word-of-mouth.

Normally, if you want to reach the general public with your message, a mass media campaign is the cornerstone. But it costs a lot of money, and at that time Yamato had little to spare for advertising. Even if we had spent heavily on advertising, it was unlikely that it would have been very effective in getting potential customers to understand what this completely new service was about.

The catch phrase "overnight delivery" clearly differentiated our product. But it was easier said than done. This is how we went about it. Collection took place during the afternoon. In the evening, the parcels would be consolidated at the bases. At 9:00 PM, they would be loaded onto long-haul trucks, which would arrive at their destination bases by the following morning. From there, parcels would be immediately distributed to the appropriate delivery centers, where the "sales drivers" (Yamato's term for the drivers of our pickup and delivery vans) would be waiting to load and deliver them to the areas for which they were responsible. The coordinated activity that made up this network depended on each link in the process: if anything went wrong at any stage, it could make overnight delivery impossible.

So the daytime hours were devoted to both delivery and collection. Transshipment between centers and bases would take place in the early morning and the evening. And all night long the long-haul trucks would be linking the bases. This coordinated activity had to be carried out on a daily basis, regardless of what the volume of freight might be. At no point could we sit on our hands because there was not enough cargo to move. Because of this, if the volume of freight was in fact low, we would definitely be running in the red. But as the volume grew, our system and its operating costs would remain the same, and if it grew a bit each day, we were on our way toward the break-even point.

Of course there were those who said, "We're charging premium rates for overnight service. But how many parcels really need to be there overnight? If we didn't promise overnight delivery, we could drop our rates, make the customers happy, send out fewer trucks, and cut down on air pollution."

However, I believed that Takkyūbin's overnight delivery would delight its users, and orders would come pouring in. If we had a large volume of freight to handle, we could keep our fees low. But if we dropped overnight delivery, this "virtuous circle" would be broken. Overnight or second-day: the shipping costs were the same. In fact, if we switched to a second-day delivery system, costs would probably increase because we'd have to add temporary storage areas for the freight.

The Odakyū Railway's "Romance Car" makes the run between Shinjuku and Hakone Yūmoto in about an hour. In order to board it you have to buy an express pass as well as a regular ticket, but that is not because its operating costs are any greater than regular train service. If you think about it from the standpoint of turnaround time, the express train is more efficient than the regular train, which takes twice as long to make a round trip. The additional fee for express service is not because the service itself actually costs more; it is the premium you pay for the convenience of greater speed.

The same is true of Takkyūbin. Just as customers delight in the convenience and efficiency of the Romance Car, they delight in the convenience of our overnight delivery.

The Goal: Overnight Delivery Everywhere

The minute we raised the banner of overnight delivery, a number of issues arose. For instance, we ought to be able to deliver overnight to any location within a given prefecture. Achieving such standardization of service was an extremely important matter for us in terms of differentiating Yamato from its competitors. If all we did was deliver overnight to the prefectural capital, it couldn't really be called overnight delivery. Only next-day service to every point in the prefecture would really allow us to make "overnight delivery" our trademark.

Take Shizuoka Prefecture, for example. Its major cities and towns are distributed along the Tōkaidō route, on a relatively flat coastal plain stretching from Mishima in the east to Lake Hamana in the west. Overnight delivery to this region fronting the Tōkaidō was only to be expected; but a fair portion of Shizuoka Prefecture's total area is taken up by the Izu Peninsula: more rugged, less accessible, full of tourist sites and fishing villages, with almost no industry of any significance. And well within range of a sightseeing day trip from Tokyo.

The main roads follow the shoreline of the peninsula, or connect across its central spine of mountains. Either way, it takes awhile to get anywhere by car or truck. But if we couldn't manage overnight delivery to the Izu Peninsula, a mere 150 kilometers from Tokyo, we might as well give up on the "overnight delivery" slogan altogether.

In every prefecture there are sparsely populated areas. Some might think it didn't really matter if deliveries to these areas took a day or so longer. In fact, all the freight companies in Japan thought that way. Many customers did too. And so did the Ministry of Transport. But I didn't.

Takkyūbin was a service assisting people's daily lives. People live in cities, but they also live in underpopulated areas and on remote islands, where they would probably like to have the same sort of convenient service available to their urban brethren. Before thinking about whether this was possible or not, we should first consider whether or not they should have such service.

My conclusion was that they should, ideally. But reality is harsh. How was this to be accomplished? The answer was simple enough: create a huge number of delivery centers. In other words, the hub-and-spoke system. If there were enough spokes in the wheel, the people within its range would all receive equal coverage. When we got to the point that we could deliver overnight anywhere in a prefecture, including remote and underpopulated areas, then we could really say that we had succeeded in differentiating our service from that of our rivals.

When we started Takkyūbin, the sides of all our delivery vans were emblazoned with our Black Cat trademark and a "Takkyūbin" logo in bold characters. They also bore the slogan "Overnight Delivery." When we opened for business in 1976, we had not yet perfected this, so I was hesitant to claim it on the sides of our vans, but I went ahead and authorized it anyway. Below, in smaller print, we added the disclaimer "Second-day service in some areas." The sides of vans and trucks had traditionally been the most important advertising medium for freight companies. Trucks driving about all day long with the company name painted on their sides were the best form of advertisement. I believed our delivery vans would also be an extremely powerful medium for advertising Takkyūbin, and I was right.

But the "Overnight Delivery" on the sides of the vans was not just for advertising purposes. It was directed at least as much at Yamato's employees, spurring them to commit themselves to delivering the kind of service we were promising.

In our first year (1976) we handled more than 1.7 million parcels. In 1977 we handled 5.4 million, an increase of 3.1 times over the previous year. In 1978 the figure was almost 10.9 million, double the preceding year. In 1979 it was almost 22.3 million, or double again. In 1980, it was 33.4, an increase of 1.5 times. In 1981 it stood at 56 million, another 1.5-fold increase.

So from the time it was launched Takkyūbin just about doubled its volume of trade every year. We had succeeded in differentiating our service. And what had made this possible was word-of-mouth from our customers.

Ramping Up to a Two-Cycle System

Our efforts toward standardization of service and implementation of overnight delivery throughout a prefecture were gradually succeeding. But as we expanded our service area, and Takkyūbin began to reach ever more remote areas, the number of locations that were getting only second-day service also began to grow. This was unavoidable. Our long-haul trucks would leave the bases around 9:00 PM and arrive at their destination bases by 7:00 AM the next morning. During that ten-hour period, running on freeways, they could average 70 kilometers an hour, but for locations more than 700 kilometers away, they could not reach the base in time to catch the delivery trucks going out on their morning rounds.

To put this in concrete terms, we could manage overnight delivery for parcels leaving Tokyo as far west as Hyōgo Prefecture; beyond that, it had to be second-day service. In other words, both Okayama and Hiroshima prefectures were getting second-day service. Now, thanks to the opening of the Shinkansen high-speed rail route, travel time from Tokyo to these prefectures had been shortened so much that travel bureaus were actually offering day trips to them. Despite this, the best we could do was second-day service. This was no good. After puzzling over this for some time, the solution I hit upon was what I called a two-cycle system.

In the beginning the Takkyūbin work cycle went like this. At the start of the day the delivery vans would load the cargo that had arrived overnight with the long-haul trucks and then set out to make their rounds. Finishing their deliveries by noon, they would then begin collection. Most of the afternoon would be devoted to this, with the vans aiming to return to their centers about 6:00 PM. After sorting the parcels by destination, the freight would then be transferred to the base, to be loaded onto the long-haul trucks for transport to the destination bases. With this, a day's work cycle ended.

What we did was change this single cycle into a two-cycle system in all its phases. In other words, the basic pattern of delivery in the morning and collection in the afternoon was revised into a double cycle in which delivery and collection both happened twice a day, morning and afternoon. And the long-distance runs linking the bases were doubled as well. Now, instead of a single departure at 9:00 PM, an earlier wave of long-haul trucks would leave at 3:00 PM.

The new Takkyūbin work cycle went like this. Parcels collected in the morning would be consolidated at the centers at noon, and transferred to the base. At the base, the parcels from the centers would be sorted by destination and loaded onto long-haul trucks for a 3:00 PM departure. The schedule for the long-haul trucks now had two distinct patterns: arrival at destination bases before 7:00 AM in order to supply the morning delivery teams, or arrival by noon in order to supply the afternoon deliveries.

Trucks arriving in the morning could have a travel time as long as sixteen hours (if they left the previous afternoon), which at an average rate of 70 kilometers an hour meant that they could reach locations as far as 1,120 kilometers away. The noon arrivals could travel for twenty-one hours if necessary, which allowed them to reach destinations 1,470 kilometers away. In the same way, parcels collected in the afternoon would be loaded onto the long-haul trucks for a 9:00 PM departure, which meant that they could run for fifteen hours, or 1,050 kilometers, before making a noon arrival.

With the adoption of this two-cycle system for collection, transport, and delivery we were able to extend the reach of our overnight deliveries to locations as far as 1,400 kilometers away from the point of departure. To put this in perspective, Hiroshima is 920 kilometers from Tokyo; Fukuoka, 1,200; and Aomori, 770.

Moreover, we were not limited to ground transport. By using air freight routes such as Chitose to Haneda and Haneda to Fukuoka, the range of overnight service was extended even further.

So Takkyūbin's service area grew steadily. By the end of March 1989 we covered 98.8 percent of Japan's total physical area, and 99.7 percent of its population. Of the 410 million parcels we delivered that year, 90.3 percent were delivered overnight, and 9.7 percent were delivered second-day.

Monitoring Service Quality

Differentiation of service was our watchword as we developed Takkyūbin, which led me to wonder if there was some way to quantify service quality.

If we couldn't express the quality of our service in concrete terms, then claiming that it was better than the rest was simply blowing our own horn. So I decided to create concrete indicators of service quality.

I had each center keep daily records of the number of packages they had been unable to deliver overnight, expressed as a percentage of the total received. Then I had a chart made displaying all the prefectures, with origins displayed on the vertical axis and destinations on the horizontal. Thus each box on the grid represented a specific pairing of originating prefecture and destination prefecture, in which was recorded the number of parcels that had failed overnight delivery, expressed as a percentage of the total number shipped between the two prefectures.

These service quality charts were published each month, making it possible to see at a glance which routes were generating problematic numbers. I thought we could then investigate the reasons why things were not going according to plan—poor communication among bases, centers, and depots, for example, or perhaps delays in transport time—and I could issue instructions on how to correct matters.

The results of this effort were disturbing. In the early days, more than 40 percent of deliveries to more remote destinations were failing to get there overnight. In general terms what this meant was that our network of bases, centers, and depots was still not functioning in a smooth and well-integrated manner. But the bad news was in one sense good news—the service quality charts I had created in order to uncover problem areas were doing their job.

Later, as our overall quality of service improved, we found it necessary to refine these service quality charts, for we discovered that the first rough versions were not as useful as they should be.

The problem was this. We could make deliveries to private homes on weekends and holidays; but businesses were generally closed on those days, with no one there to receive deliveries. Thus a package shipped on Friday could not be delivered until Monday, and this was inflating the number of parcels that "failed" to make their destination overnight. So we had to correct for this.

Moreover, if packages returned to the centers because of a business holiday, or packages that were being held at centers for various reasons, including those awaiting specified delivery dates, were not excluded from our general calculations, it would throw all our data off. So I had two different charts made and published: the first, uncorrected, representing all freight we were handling; the second, a revised version generated after excluding items in certain specific categories.

At present we are not only continuing this monthly monitoring and report of service quality for Takkyūbin operations in general, we have also added a special report on our refrigerated transport service, "Cool Takkyūbin."

Cool Takkyūbin was rolled out as a new nationwide service in 1988. We now offer both refrigerated (approximately 37° F) and frozen (approximately 0° F) service, and the number of users continues to grow rapidly (see chapter 12 for details). Obviously, the important thing with Cool Takkyūbin is that it stay cool—so we needed to be able to monitor whether or not the required temperature ranges were being met. At this point our monthly report of general Takkyūbin service quality is accompanied by an assessment of the failure rate of temperature control for Cool Takkyūbin.

As you might expect, the difficulty of such temperature control varies with the season. In winter it is usually easy to keep both refrigerated and frozen cargo within the required temperature ranges. In Hokkaidō, however, where winter temperatures can drop into the teens or lower, it is sometimes necessary to take special precautions to prevent refrigerated goods from freezing.

In summer, when it is common for temperatures to rise into the 80s and sometimes higher, careful monitoring is required to maintain specified temperature ranges. Once ice cream has softened, it can't be refrozen without damaging its quality.

Service quality monitoring is an absolutely essential task in our efforts to implement the Takkyūbin strategy of differentiation of service.

Provider's Mind, User's Mind

This is a story from the days before we had refined and perfected our service quality charts.

It was one of our monthly meetings at which service quality was on the agenda for discussion. I had just hurled a thunderbolt or two, angered by the fact that service was not improving, despite the fact that I was talking myself blue in the face about the need to differentiate our service from that of our competitors. It was not just that parcels to remote areas were arriving late—the numbers were poor even in our own backyard, the twenty-three wards of central Tokyo. I was really irritated.

One of the executives responsible for monitoring field operations responded to this by saying, "We're unloading the morning arrivals quite quickly, so by noon we're usually through with deliveries."

"What in the world are you talking about?!" I shouted. "Right now the failure rate for overnight delivery is in double digits!"

"Yamato Transport is attempting to deliver every morning. But we are finding that a lot of the recipients are not at home, and taking the packages back to the centers for second-day delivery," he explained.

"OK, OK," I growled. "I guess if the customers aren't home there's nothing we can do. Let's give some thought to how we should treat these instances when we are computing our failure rates." And that concluded this little scene.

Yet for days afterward, this issue continued to bother me so much that I had trouble sleeping. Then it hit me.

Yamato's employees were basically assuming that it was the customer's fault if he or she were not home to receive the parcels they were working so hard to deliver. But was this really the case? The customer's response might go something like this: "It wasn't like I was gone all day. I'd just stepped out for a minute to run a few errands when the delivery van showed up. It's their fault." So we have two completely different versions of the problem.

I thought about this. The mind of the service provider and the mind of the user are often diametrically opposed. The provider tends to think of things from his own point of view; in other words, in terms of his own convenience. But this is a mistake.

Customers often grumble about the service at restaurants. The proprietors may say, "We give our staff very strict instructions regarding how they should relate to customers," but as we all know, it is a quite common occurrence to see waiters and waitresses so lost in chatting with each other that they are completely oblivious to customers trying to get their attention.

I gave serious thought to ways of dealing with the problem of customers not being at home when our vans arrived. They couldn't be expected to sit at home all day. There are plenty of families in which both husband and wife are at work during the day. We surveyed some large apartment complexes and found that in about 40 percent of the households no one was at home during the daytime.

So what were we to do? Instead of thinking of this as a problem of absent customers, I began to think of it in terms of at-home delivery. I believed it was Yamato's responsibility to make sure that we called when the customer was at home. If they were gone during the day, that meant showing up again in the evening. Working men and women frequently would not arrive at home until after seven o'clock. So it seemed to me we needed to make night deliveries as well.

In the beginning, I had set 6:00 PM as the cutoff for both pickup and delivery, so I decided to extend delivery hours to 8:00 PM (at present, 9:00 PM). And as soon as we began to observe this principle of "at-home delivery," our performance in terms of overnight deliveries increased dramatically.

Service vs. Costs

There is always a trade-off between service and costs. If you raise the level of service, costs go up; if you keep costs down, service suffers. The job of the business executive is to keep this problem constantly in mind, and decide which should be prioritized in any given situation.

When we were launching Takkyūbin, I decided that service would come first, then profits. I reasoned that if we did not achieve a level of service high enough to differentiate us from the postal service and other potential rivals, we weren't going to be making any profits anyway.

This sort of thinking must be applied to capital investment and employment issues as well. At Yamato our slogan was people and trucks first, then freight—in other words, we put a priority on expanding the number of our employees and vehicles, since our market was not going to expand if they could not stay ahead of the volume of freight we were handling. I was determined to develop latent demand by being ready to meet it with sufficient personnel and equipment to provide a high level of service.

First Service, Then Profits

At Yamato Transport, before we started Takkyūbin, we used to have a monthly operations meeting with the heads of all the field offices. After we introduced a computerized system, monthly financial figures for each office were available on the thirteenth of the following month, so we had this meeting on or about the fifteenth in order to review and analyze the data.

After we launched Takkyūbin, we continued to have these monthly operations meetings. But I stopped putting a review of the figures from each field office on the agenda. Since they were bound to be running in the red for some time, it seemed pointless.

Instead, we discussed service quality. I began the first meeting after the launch by saying, "From now on, I am taking the financials off the agenda—all I want to hear about is the level of service."

My reasoning was that in order to pull out of the red, we had to increase the volume of freight, and the only way I could see to do that was to use the quality of our service to differentiate us from our rivals.

As I said, service and costs are a trade-off. Improve service and you will increase costs. Cut costs, and you will find yourself cutting back on service as well. As an example, let's assume you create a service center for collections and deliveries in an underpopulated area. Naturally, from the get-go you are faced with fixed expenses such as leasing the facility, and an increase in trucking expenses in order to transfer the freight between your new center and its base. Personnel expenses will increase by at least the salary of the center's manager. (Let's assume for the moment that you don't have to hire any new drivers, and that the increase in efficiency in pickup and delivery as a result of the new center may even cut costs a bit.) In any case, your overall expenses are going to increase. On the other hand, the center will make overnight delivery to this area possible, resulting in a dramatic improvement in service.

Improved service is a plus. Increased costs are a minus. This is the trade-off you always run up against as a manager. You weigh the pluses and minuses, and if the balance comes out positive, then you go ahead and set up your new service center. Or at least that's the standard answer. But is it in fact the correct one?

The positive effect of upgrading service is realized through increased sales. However, there are many factors determining gross sales—accurately measuring how much of an increase in sales is attributable to any one variable is quite difficult. Increased costs, on the other hand, can be quantified with relative precision, but when you think of the time and manpower involved in the task of assembling and interpreting such data, to do so seems likely just to add to your costs.

This is precisely why, at the first operations meeting after starting Takkyūbin, I stressed that I would say nothing about the financials, but would pursue the issue of service tenaciously. At the meeting, I gave my managerial team a slogan that encapsulated what I thought: "First service, then profits." And I declared that I wanted them to adhere to it like holy scripture.

Was setting up a new service center a plus or a minus? We didn't have the time to toy with such questions. Once we had launched Takkyūbin, we had to move a certain volume of freight to break even—anything less and we ran in the red. So the prime directive was to do whatever was necessary to increase the density of freight as soon as possible. In such a situation, it was ridiculous to think of quitting simply because of rising costs. Service and costs are a trade-off, but it is not a question of comparing them and choosing one or the other. The question is which to prioritize.

So I told my managers that I didn't want them wasting their time trying to figure out the relative merits of service versus the costs involved. Instead, I wanted them to think about nothing other than how to improve service—and then just do it. Thus the motto "First service, then profits."

An example. During the lengthy period of Yamato Transport's declining performance, I had stressed again and again the need to watch our operating expenses. In the trucking business, a lot of long-distance phone calls are made in order to maintain communication between field offices. But I had directed my field managers to keep an eye on their staff, and encourage them to use inter-office mail instead of long-distance phone calls, since we had trucks running between the offices all the time.

Now, I reversed this policy. At a meeting I told my managers that I wanted the sales drivers to feel free to make long-distance phone calls whenever they needed to. If they were unable to find an address for a delivery, I wanted them to call the sender directly to confirm the address. You'd be surprised at how many addresses are written incorrectly. Even if it were the customer's mistake, returning a parcel as undeliverable because the address cannot be located is the pits as far as service is concerned. Even if the sender corrects the address and sends it out again, the package ends up arriving at least a couple of days late.

There was opposition to this plan on the grounds that the telephone calls would end up costing more than the delivery fee for the parcels, but to me the merits of keeping our promise of overnight delivery and making the customers happy were worth far more than whatever the phone calls cost.

When I introduced the two-cycle system for managing our collection, transport, and delivery schedules, it also made me give serious thought to the trade-off between service and costs. I have already touched on this in chapter 6, but let me add a few more words here.

At first, collection and delivery were on a single daily cycle. The parcels to be delivered arrived in the morning, so mornings were given over to deliveries. And since the long-haul trucks were normally dispatched at night, the collection of the parcels to fill them was done in the afternoons. But this way of thinking was a holdover from our days of handling commercial freight, and I finally realized that it was not really appropriate to a home parcel service responding to the needs of individuals.

With commercial freight, you are dealing with businesses—manufacturers or vendors—that keep normal daytime hours. Arriving freight is needed for the day's business, so you deliver it in the morning; departing freight is shipped as a product of the day's business and is collected in the afternoon. This pattern holds true pretty much everywhere in the country.

On the other hand, with home deliveries, if the delivery is going to be used in making that evening's dinner, then it might be nice to have it in the morning, but if it arrives by 3:00 in the afternoon or so, that is probably fine. As for collection, there are many cases in which the customer has prepared the parcel the evening before and would like it picked up in the morning. In other words, the pattern does not necessarily conform to the formula of deliveries in the morning and collection in the afternoon.

With the two-cycle system for pickup and delivery, costs do not go up very much, and service improves considerably. So far, so good. But doubling the long-haul runs is another matter. You are moving the same volume of freight overall, so the revenue is the same, but your transport costs are doubled. This is a serious problem. I decided to go ahead with the two-cycle system anyway, because it was necessary in order to extend the range of our overnight service from 700 kilometers to 1,000 kilometers.

If our strategy of differentiation of service worked its magic and the volume of freight doubled, then it stood to reason that we would actually need two long-haul shipments a day. Rather than using two trucks to haul them both at 9:00 PM, it made sense to stagger the departure times to 3:00 PM and 9:00 PM, so that one truck could do the work of two. That way, costs should remain pretty much the same while service significantly improved.

My thinking with regard to at-home delivery was much the same. When I extended the delivery schedule from 6:00 PM to 8:00 PM, I got complaints from the personnel department. Because of regulations regarding working hours, part-time drivers would have to be employed to take over from our regular staff. Personnel thought it would be difficult to hire such substitute drivers, but this turned out not to be the case. There were plenty of applicants. I was amused when I learned that in one case, out in the country somewhere, a post office employee had secretly applied to moonlight in one of these positions.

So the problem was not hiring, it was the increase in wages we had to pay—and the personnel department was worried. Next month we're going to need several billion yen more to meet payroll! Is that what you want? I said to them, "The increase in drivers' wages doesn't bother me—the waste of money is the salary of whoever in personnel is coming up with such figures!" If we were truly going to put service first and worry about profits later, we could do without such calculations.

First Trucks, Then Freight

From the time of its launch Takkyūbin was a hit with consumers, and I sensed a solidity to the growth in the volume of freight we were handling. This growth forced us to rapidly expand our area of service, adding thirty to fifty service centers a year. Of course this was up-front investment, predicated on the continuing expansion of our volume of freight.

But there were also centers that we built because certain service areas were so large that a single truck could not cover them, even though the volume of freight they generated was small. Normally the actual level of freight being handled by an area was what determined the number of trucks assigned to it, but in these cases, even when the number of parcels per day might number a hundred or fewer, we might assign two or three trucks to it anyway.

My thinking on this was that as long as we were building the centers, then even in underpopulated areas there would ideally be a minimum of five trucks assigned to each of them, and that was what I instructed my staff. One truck for each point of the compass—north, south, east, and west—and one for the center. With only two trucks, for instance, customers in the east and west might get morning delivery, but those in the north and south would have to wait until afternoon. With two more trucks assigned, north and south would get morning delivery as well.

The customers would realize this right away: as service improved, they would respond to it, and the amount of freight we handled from this area would grow. Thus the fifth truck, for the center. And that, I told my people, was the minimum we should be aiming for.

In establishing a new center, it would take a lot of work to determine the projected number of parcels to be handled per truck, and all the costs involved. In any case, projected figures are often unreliable. Since we were introducing a completely new service to a new region, any predictions about how things would go once we commenced business were necessarily pretty rough, and would no doubt change frequently as time went by. In my opinion, costs change on a daily basis.

Since there seemed little point in making plans based on an analysis of costs, it seemed to me the only thing we could do was think about how to provide the best service. So five trucks. Why not? At least we'd have all the bases covered, and a player in reserve. Even if there wasn't enough freight to keep them busy, the sight of five trucks running around the area would serve as collateral advertising, and help get people in the mood to send parcels. If we could simply get the local people to start saying, "Look, there's the Takkyūbin truck coming up the hill. Must be almost ten o'clock," then we would have them as customers eventually.

And in fact, within a year or so of establishing a center in a remote area, the couple of trucks that began by running around nearly empty would be coming in with full loads even when there were five trucks, and then ten. I was now able to say "Trucks first, freight later" with the confidence born of experience.

Why Hire More People?

At the end of fiscal 1976, the year Yamato Transport launched Takkyūbin, we had 5,650 employees. Five years later, at the end of fiscal 1981, we had 9,270, and ten years later, at the end of fiscal 1986, their number had swelled to 23,600. We had added 3,620 employees in the first five years and 14,320 in the second, for a ten-year total of 17,950 new employees.

Now, in March 1999, Yamato's employees number 74,888—making it the third largest corporate employer in Japan after NTT and JR East. Both of the latter were initially government-operated monopolies, so among pure private-sector firms, Yamato is the largest in Japan in terms of the size of its staff.

In any case, this was remarkable growth. And it didn't happen by accident. We made it happen.

It's easy for a freight company executive to improve service. All he has to do is hire more people. Freight is a labor-intensive industry, and the more people you have working, the better the service will be. Since the majority of these employees are truck drivers, if you are going to hire more of them you also have to provide more trucks for them to drive. The more trucks and drivers you have, the better you are able to respond quickly and effectively to consumer demand.

This was certainly true of Takkyūbin. More employees meant a more powerful collection and delivery force. And this meant a rapid expansion in the volume of freight we were handling.

Let's look at the relationship between the expansion in hiring I have just detailed and the expansion in the volume of freight Takkyūbin was handling. In 1976 Takkyūbin carried 1.75 million parcels. By 1981 this had jumped to 50.6 million, and in 1986 to 239.8 million parcels.

Taking 1976 as the base, by 1981 the number of our employees had increased 1.6 times, while the volume of freight had increased 29.6 times; by 1986, the number of employees had increased 4.1 times, while the volume of freight had expanded by 140.2 times.

Without a doubt, "First people, then freight."

Everything in creation has merits and demerits. All human affairs have their good and bad sides.

Many managers are afraid of the increased personnel costs that come with increased hiring. They are fixated on the demerits of the situation. When we hear about policies geared to restoring the health of a company, or about corporate restructuring, they usually center on cutting staff. But I have always had my doubts about this.

Why do companies employ people in the first place? To make things, or to sell things—to carry out the tasks the company was established to perform. So what is demanded of the employees is that they demonstrate the ability to make or sell the things they are supposed to. In recent times the trend toward automation—having machines do the work that people once did—has been strong; but there are still plenty of things that only people can do, or that people can still do better. The greatest merit of human workers is their skills and their contribution to increased productivity, and these must be the core issues in thinking about human resources.

Increased personnel costs are a demerit of hiring more employees, but before worrying about that, we should consider the merits of increased productivity and revenues that the new employees will bring to the company. If these merits did not exist, there wouldn't be any point in hiring more people. Yet by refusing to hire more people because of the increase in personnel costs, a company runs the risk of losing its momentum.

In corporate management, the issue of people is the biggest issue. Corporations are recognized as a social entity because of the work of their people. An entrepreneur who thinks he can ignore human issues and pay attention only to return on investment ought to give up being an entrepreneur, in my opinion. If your business is not making some contribution to society through the labor of your employees, then it is pretty much meaningless as a social entity, it seems to me.

My slogan "First service, then profits" does not mean I am uninterested in profits. What it really means is that if you stop thinking about profits first, and instead concentrate your energies on providing the best possible service, profits will inevitably come your way.

If you think only about profits, and don't concern yourself much with service, you can't achieve differentiation of service, and your revenues are not going to increase. As a result, you will never see the profits you desire. It's a vicious cycle.

There are pluses and minuses to all this, whatever way you think about it. Management is always a matter of trade-offs. One of the biggest responsibilities of the corporate manager is to come up with the most appropriate response to these trade-offs.

However, if it's a middle manager, not the company president, who is going around saying "First service, then profits," he's likely to get chewed out pretty harshly by the boss So you don't care about profits? Do you care about your job?

"First service, then profits" is something only the president can say. And that's why he is the one who has to say it.

Safety First, Business Second

As I related in chapter 1, soon after joining Yamato Transport I fell ill and had to quit work. Four years later I had recovered and was sent to manage a subsidiary of ours, Shizuoka Transport. The story I am about to tell is from that time. Shizuoka Transport was a company that had gone into receivership, and the bank had asked Yamato to take over its management.

This was 1955, so there was no bullet train, no superhighways. The Tōkaidō highway still ran along its old route. Our trucks were old, our facilities inadequate. There were a fair number of traffic accidents due to this, and frequent on-the-job injuries. Nowadays forklifts and other machinery are the norm in the workplace, but back then, a poor trucking company had to rely on raw manpower for the loading and unloading of freight, and people got hurt.

One day, we got a summons from the Labor Standards Inspection Office. As general affairs manager, it was my responsibility to respond to the summons. When I got there, the chief inspector said to me, "Shizuoka Transport has more accidents by far than any company under my jurisdiction. If I can't get you to cooperate with me in reducing the number of accidents, I'll have to subject you to special inspection. I have a model company in my jurisdiction. I'd like to have you go take a look at it."

The model company turned out to be a wood-processing factory. There were a lot of them in Shizuoka, and they were known for having a lot of accidents related to the saws and other machinery. I really wondered how much of a model the place was going to provide for someone in the transport industry, but I thought it would be bad to ignore the inspector's advice, so I went and visited the place.

The factory had no fancy facilities, and there was no evidence they were making any big investment in safety, but when I listened to what the owner had to say, I was deeply impressed.

According to him, safety had mostly to do with the owner's attitude. One of the factory walls displayed a large Green Cross flag, the symbol for workplace safety in Japan. You would see this in almost any workplace. What was different was an enormous poster filling another wall that said "Safety First, Productivity Second."

The owner said, "Before, we really had a lot of workplace accidents. But I began thinking about the preciousness of human life, and felt I absolutely had to do something to cut down on them. And it occurred to me that as long as all I was doing was demanding increased productivity, the accidents were going to keep happening."

So he distilled this feeling into the slogan "Safety first, productivity second" and posted it on the shop wall. "As time went by," he said, "safety gradually improved—without any significant drop in productivity. When I was telling them to put the same priority on safety and productivity, we weren't doing very well at either."

What the factory owner had said hit home with me. Now I understood why the chief inspector had wanted me to pay this visit. As soon as I got back from the factory, I called Shizuoka Transport's executives together and declared that from that point on our work would be guided by the motto "Safety first, business second."

At the time, Shizuoka Transport was making regularly scheduled daily runs between Shizuoka and Tokyo. The work schedule for the drivers went something like this. Arrive at work at 1:00 PM to do freight collection, leaving with a fully loaded truck from the Shizuoka terminal at about 7:00 PM. Drop off freight at various depots along the way, and arrive in Tokyo early the next morning. Unload freight at the terminal, make deliveries, and be done with work about 10:00 AM. Catch a nap in a field office bunkroom, and start the return trip about 3:00 PM, arriving in Shizuoka the next morning. Make the final round of deliveries, and punch out about 10:00 AM and go home to sleep. This pattern of three workdays with two nights on the road was pretty much standard. However, there were many times when the work load was heavy enough that drivers just returning from one of these three-day trips were asked to turn around and go back out again—which meant four nights on the road and not getting off work until the fifth day. This was called a "dragonfly return" (from a Japanese expression meaning a round trip with only a brief stopover). It answered the company's shortage of drivers, and gave the drivers a chance at greater earnings from overtime pay, so the dragonfly return had become a company habit.

One cause of industrial accidents is overwork. That was clear. So one way of reducing accidents was to avoid forcing employees into a position where they were working impossibly long overtime hours and night shifts. The intent of my "Safety first, business second" slogan was to tell the employees to refuse assignments that would lead to overwork, despite what managers might be asking them to do. In concrete terms, I wanted to put an end to the dragonfly return. That would be a start.

I had "Safety First, Business Second" posters displayed all over the company. By putting business second, I wanted to really stress that safety came first. Sure enough, accidents slowly declined. And business? If anything, better than before.

When I had finished my assignment in Shizuoka and returned to Yamato Transport's main offices in Tokyo, I was shocked by Yamato's high accident rate. With a fleet of about three thousand trucks at that point, we were having nearly five hundred accidents a year (though this number was inflated by the inclusion of even minor fender-benders in Yamato's depots).

So I immediately brought out the "Safety first, business second" slogan again, and began a work-safety campaign. After a few years the accident rate began to fall off, and by the time our fleet had reached five thousand trucks, we were having fewer than a hundred accidents annually.

You cannot find a factory in Japan where the "Safety First" slogan is not displayed. Yet it has become such a cliché that I seriously doubt it has much effect. Why? Because what comes second is never mentioned.

Every year, at the beginning of each quarter, stern orders come from the top that the goal is to increase sales by 10 percent over the year before, and this goal must be met. Yet halfway through the year, with this goal almost met, it is discovered that profits are down. So the order goes out that the focus should be on raising profits, even if sales suffer and unprofitable lines must be abandoned.

Every year National Safety Month rolls around, and of course the order "Safety First" comes down from on high. But when there are complaints about the merchandise, this suddenly becomes a demand to put "Quality First." There are a lot of company bosses who like to order a lot of different things put first.

Doesn't this just go to show that without second, there really isn't any first?

A company president for whom everything is first is operating at the tactical level. A president who can clearly indicate what comes first and what comes second in terms of the actual situation of his company is operating at the strategic level.

The role of the company president is to analyze the present situation of his company, decide what should be prioritized, and explain this in a logical manner to his employees. In other words, it begins and ends with strategic thinking.

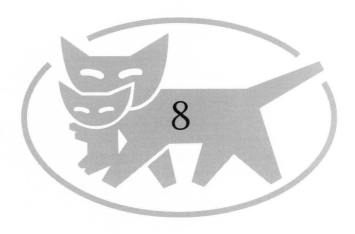

8

Frontrunner's Plans and Battles with the Bureaucracy

This chapter recounts the process by which Takkyūbin stayed ahead of its competitors and overcame bureaucratic red tape in order to continue its growth.

Noting the success of Takkyūbin, a number of our competitors entered the home parcel delivery market. To establish a commanding lead over these latecomers, we implemented a series of three "Frontrunner" three-year plans aimed at building our national network and achieving nationwide overnight delivery. There is no end to upgrading service. Once you have achieved one goal, you must move on to the next—ahead of the rest of the pack. That is how a company keeps on winning.

But there was a major obstacle to the construction of the nationwide network we needed in order to keep improving our service: the inefficient licensing and approval bureaucracy of the Ministry of Transport. Moreover, bound as we were by antiquated legal restraints, we had difficulty implementing the unique pricing structure so important to Takkyūbin. I fought the bureaucracy head-on, with lawsuits and a newspaper advertising campaign, won the support of public opinion, and eventually got what we were asking for. Private-sector companies should never give in to unnecessary regulation without a fight.

Profitability at the Five-Year Mark

When I launched Takkyūbin in 1976, it was over the objections of most of the people in the company. But once we got underway, Yamato's employees showed their dedication by quickly getting a handle on what this new line of work required and putting together a system to handle it. However, unlike commercial freight, it was a matter of collection and delivery of single parcels, making every day a difficult struggle to increase the efficiency of our operations.

One thing we noticed right away was that unlike the high-handed treatment we had become accustomed to from commercial freight clients and their employees, housewives were always ready with a cheerful greeting and a thank you when we came round for pickups or deliveries. Unused to such pleasantries, our drivers were quite moved to be treated in this way. Never having realized that their work was valued so highly, they all spoke of how happy this made them, and how it made their jobs more satisfying.

Even the employees who had complained at first about what a hassle parcel delivery was compared to the big commercial freight shipments of appliances they were used to handling now began to complain less and less.

In the world of the truck driver, driving a big rig has more bragging rights than driving a little delivery van, and when we started Takkyūbin, veteran tractor-trailer drivers hated the idea of having to drive the vans. But as time went by they actually began to volunteer for such duty.

It was taxing work, but the response from the customers made up for it: in 1976 we carried only 1.7 million parcels, but after that the figures rose explosively to 5.4 million in 1977, 18.8 million in 1978, and 22.26 million in 1979. The effect of the differentiation of service we had achieved by hammering away at the slogan "First service, then profits" was immense.

I was delighted by how well Takkyūbin was doing, but there were things in the air that made me wonder how bright the future might be for Yamato Transport as a whole.

In February 1979 we withdrew completely from delivery operations for the Mitsukoshi department store chain. There were many similarities between this department store delivery business and Takkyūbin, and it was certainly not an operation that could be lightly dismissed. Moreover, we owed Mitsukoshi an enormous debt of gratitude for becoming one of our first dependable clients in the early days of the company, more than a half century before. But as I explained in the prologue, Yamato Transport had suffered under the high-handed management of Mitsukoshi's President Okada for too long, and we had come to the point that we could no longer do business in partnership with him or his company. It was the steady growth of Takkyūbin that helped stiffen my resolve to part company with Mitsukoshi.

In 1979 there was another major event affecting our business. That was the dissolution of our business relationship with Matsushita Electric. After the war, Yamato was slow to enter the long-haul trucking business, but when we finally got our route license for the Tōkaidō in 1960 and started up operations in Osaka, we began to transport goods for a number of Matsushita's divisions. They became our largest client.

But this high-volume transport of electrical appliances was about as far from Takkyūbin as you could get. On the one hand you had linear long-distance transport of shipments comprised of hundreds of units; on the other, dispersed transport and delivery of individual small parcels—the two types of operation were polar opposites. There is an old saying that if you chase two rabbits you won't catch either one, and it seemed to apply here. If we continued to try to do both, we would do neither well.

From the time we started Takkyūbin I had instructed our people in the field to gradually reduce the volume of large commercial freight transactions. But it was hard for them to break ties to clients that had been built up over many years, nor were they confident that Takkyūbin was going to fill the revenue void left by dissolving such relationships—so the fact of the matter was that for the most part my instructions were not carried out.

There were many at Yamato who thought we ought to continue with both services—Takkyūbin was doing a great job, but what was the point to cutting off the commercial freight clients we had worked so hard to establish? But I had literally bet the firm on Takkyūbin. I had no idea whether it would succeed or fail, but I knew one thing for sure: if we couldn't make it work, the company would go under. And the way to make it work was to be ruthless about sticking to this one type of business.

I felt terrible about it, but I decided to cease all business transactions with the commercial clients to whom we owed so much. And I went in person to Matsushita Electric, our biggest client, to express my gratitude for their many years of patronage, but also to ask them to dissolve their business relationship with us.

The Matsushita executive I spoke with was pretty startled. He was used to having shipping company reps coming to him on an almost daily basis, trying to establish a relationship with Matsushita—and here I was, trying to get out of one! But I explained Yamato's position and the nature of the Takkyūbin enterprise in some detail, and said that among other things, we were going to be downsizing the trucks in our fleet and would no longer be able to deliver the kind of service Matsushita required. I apologized for the inconvenience, and in the end Matsushita was gracious about accepting what I had to say.

The loss of a major client is no small thing for a company. There was ample reason to believe that this might cause disquiet among Yamato's employees—especially since cutting off the relationship from our side was such an unusual thing to do. It couldn't have been done without confidence and decisiveness at the top. Or, to put it another way, some things can *only* be decided at the top. And in those cases, the company president has an obligation to give a clear explanation to his employees of what he is doing and why he is doing it. In the case of Mitsukoshi, the employees were delighted with the decision. And with Matsushita as well, they took the news positively and pledged their cooperation in making Takkyūbin work.

The loss of Mitsukoshi and Matsushita as clients resulted in our LTL trucking division—which was responsible for both commercial freight and Takkyūbin—running almost ¥500 million in the red in the 1979 fiscal year, while pretax earnings for the company as a whole declined sharply to 86 percent of the previous year.

At the same time, the loss of these long-established commercial clients did its part to galvanize the company—once they knew they were fighting with their backs to the wall, our employees threw themselves into making Takkyūbin work.

As a result, the number of parcels handled by Takkyūbin in 1980 was 33.4 million, up 150 percent over the preceding year. Gross sales amounted to some ¥69.9 billion, and pretax revenues were ¥3.9 billion, giving us a pretax profit margin of 5.6 percent!

We were finally making it over the hump into profitability. It had been an intense five years since launching Takkyūbin and, in all honesty, we'd reached this goal quicker than I'd thought. The employees were confident, pumped-up, full of fight.

A virtuous circle had begun.

The Frontrunner's Three-Year Plan

With Takkyūbin, Yamato Transport had achieved a profit margin of 5.6 percent. This news rocked the trucking industry.

"I can't understand why they want to get into this Takkyūbin business. Everybody knows it's bound to lose money. If they go ahead with it, Yamato Transport's going to go down the drain." No one actually said it, but everyone must have been thinking it. And now it was turning a profit. A 5.6 percent profit, at that.

However, they soon surprised us even more than we surprised them—in no time, there was a rash of Takkyūbin wannabes. Thirty-five companies in all.

What made Yamato successful was the fact that we had targeted the ordinary housewife, whom no one had given any thought to before, as our freight customer.

"Huh. Come to think of it, housewives probably make good customers; they don't haggle over rates. And if you look at Yamato's numbers, it looks like a pretty good market. We better get in before the competition." All the other companies seemed to be thinking along these lines.

They also appear to have thought that one of the secrets of Yamato's success was our Black Cat Yamato ad campaign on TV. So now thirty-five companies, each with their own animal trademark, began to flood the media. Dogs, bears, lions, elephants, giraffes: you name it, there they were. It was beginning to feel a bit like Noah's ark, and just as crowded.

It's a bit of a digression, but I should tell you the story of Yamato's trademark. Familiar at this point to almost everyone in Japan, Yamato's Black Cat trademark was originally inspired by America's Allied Van Lines, which used to use a calico cat as its trademark.

In 1957 Yamato teamed up with Allied to handle moving the household goods of U.S. military personnel between Japan and the United States. My father Yasuomi, then president of the company, was quite taken with the message of the trademark, which implied that the company would be as careful and dependable with the customer's belongings as a mother cat with its kittens. So he got permission from Allied to use the idea, and had a new logo designed based on a drawing by a child of one of our employees.

Aggressive use of the Black Cat mark dramatically raised the Japanese public's awareness of Takkyūbin, and definitely contributed to the growth of our sales. But that did that mean that all you had to do to catch up with Yamato in the parcel business was to come up with a similar animal trademark? Of course not.

Actually, I was more bemused than surprised by the sudden influx of competitors. Parcel delivery is a network business. To get into it without a solid network seemed either stupid or foolhardy, and I was taken aback by the nerve the other companies were displaying.

Imitation of the successful is one of the ingrained habits of the Japanese. When they heard that Yamato was succeeding with the home parcel operations that everyone had said would never make anybody any money, you would think they would look into the reasons why. Or at least realize that there was more to it than simply being a hit with the housewives because of a cute trademark.

All the same, Yamato could not afford to be complacent. If new entries into the market failed, that was their problem. But they had all been in the trucking business for many years, and even if they did not have much of a network, practically any of them should be able to manage overnight delivery between Tokyo and wherever their headquarters was located. Moreover, there were thirty-five of them. Ignoring them, or underestimating their potential impact on Takkyūbin, was out of the question. To me, this situation made it even more imperative to proceed with differentiating our service from theirs.

So in April 1981, I launched a three-year plan intended to carry us through fiscal 1984. I invited the employees to name the plan, and the winner, out of 1,833 responses, was Frontrunner's Three-Year Plan, proposed by one of our female employees. Since the goal of the plan was differentiation of service, I thought this was a wonderful name, conjuring up as it did the image of a top marathon runner pulling ahead of the pack in the final stage of a marathon, and suddenly finding himself alone, with no rival anywhere near.

We were aiming at keeping our service ahead of the pack with this three-year plan, with three concrete goals:

1. Completion of Takkyūbin's national network
2. Expansion of the overnight delivery zones
3. Creation of a sales and operations system to achieve goals 1 and 2

The national network for Takkyūbin at the time of its launch was in reality a service area centered on the Kantō region, covering only 3.4 percent of Japan's total land area and 25.4 percent of its population. This had grown to include the Tōkaidō and Sanyōdō regions, as well as northern Kyūshū, so that at the inception of the three-year plan we covered 31 percent of the country and 78 percent of its population. But this was still far from being the genuine national network we were aiming for. Hobbled by the licensing system for trucking operations, we finally succeeded in reaching 80 percent of Japan's total area in fiscal 1984.

Our efforts with regard to overnight delivery began with revamping our system for monitoring service, and setting new standards. The first thing that had to be tackled was establishment of a data management system for logging and tracking parcels as they moved through the system. We had already introduced a system of bar codes on the waybills, and online management of this data, but it needed to be further refined and upgraded.

By 1984 our data management had come a long way, but efforts to expand our overnight delivery zones were producing few visible results. On the other hand, we had now implemented full service on Sundays and holidays, and delivery times were steadily growing shorter. And in terms of creating the internal business and operational structure we needed to support our growth, we had established a new base in the Hanshin region and moved ahead in a few other areas, but our progress was far from dramatic. In short, after three years we were still far from the goals we had set, and I decided to create a second three-year plan.

When you set a goal to achieve a certain level of service, it seems foreordained that once you have attained that goal it becomes the new norm, and you have to move on to implementing newer and higher levels of service.

The second three-year plan was dubbed The New Frontrunner's Three-Year Plan and implemented between fiscal 1984 and fiscal 1986. Reflecting on our failure to achieve most of the goals set out in the first three-year plan, we were determined this time to offer service worthy of a frontrunner.

With the introduction of the two-cycle system, the area reached by overnight delivery expanded significantly. And the extension of delivery hours to make sure we provided at-home delivery to customers was also producing positive results. In addition, our tracking system took a major step forward with the introduction of portable point-of-sale terminals carried by our sales drivers, giving us a powerful new tool for monitoring and improving our delivery times.

So our second Frontrunner plan achieved impressive improvements in our level of service—though our push to complete our nationwide network was stalled by the inflexibility of the Ministry of Transport.

So I decided to initiate another three-year plan for the period from fiscal 1987 to fiscal 1989. This time we named it Frontrunner's Three-Year Plan, Part III, sticking with the frontrunner concept. The goal was still differentiation of service, but the change from the two previous plans was that we set quantitative goals. Before, I had wanted to emphasize the qualitative aspects of the plans, and had held back on setting specific figures as benchmarks. But now I felt to really become a balanced, excellent company, quantitative goals were indispensable.

In concrete terms, it worked out like this:

1. Profitability: Pretax profits of 5 percent or better
2. Scale: Net sales of at least ¥340 billion
3. Financial soundness: equity ratio (percentage of shareholders' equity to total assets) of 50 percent or better
4. Employee benefits: at least 100 days off per annum

The reason I included employee benefits in the plan was because I felt that in order to deliver excellent service to our customers, our employees needed some time to enjoy their own lives. I thought two days off each week would ensure this, but I also had to consider maintaining our level of service and holding the line against rising costs. So for practical purposes I decided that gradually increasing the number of vacation days was the most realistic approach, and set a minimum of a hundred days a year as our current goal.

In the end we achieved two out of the four goals of the plan: scale and employee benefits. Net sales totaled ¥370 billion, but our pretax profits stalled at 2.3 percent.

We also made great progress with our nationwide network after an epic struggle with the bureaucracy, but I will describe this in detail later.

Our three Frontrunner plans had taken us through nine years of growth, but we still had not come as far as I would have liked. The excellent service I set as our goal seemed elusive, like a mirage that continually recedes as you approach it. I suppose another way to put it is that the goal is never-ending. To keep providing new levels of service, you must always keep moving forward.

Our Battle with the Ministry of Transport

One of the central goals of the Frontrunner plans was the completion of a nationwide Takkyūbin network. When we started Takkyūbin our network was heavily weighted towards the Kantō region, which meant that while we covered 25 percent of the country's population, we were reaching only 3.4 percent of its total area.

At the time, licenses were required to operate freight trucking operations, and we needed licensing that would allow us to operate nationwide. But getting new licenses was a very difficult task.

Until December 1989 trucking operations were regulated by the Road Transportation Law. This law treated freight and passenger transport in the same way. Less-than-truckload (LTL) carriers collecting freight from the general public were regulated in the same manner as tour buses.

For example, you needed a route license for every road you traveled. This might make sense for a long-distance bus, but for freight transport, did it really matter whether we used Highway 1, Highway 246, or the Tōmei Expressway? Yet there we were, wrapped up in red tape that demanded we specify and get a license for every road we used.

If you had a license for Highway 1, you could establish a field office in any of the towns along its route, but not in the hinterland beyond. Freight collection and delivery was officially permitted within a three-kilometer radius of your office, though this three-kilometer limit was not actually specified in the law. And in fact, there was a tacit understanding that for collection and delivery purposes, this radius might be stretched to ten or even twenty kilometers. So if you had a route license, most of the cities, towns, and villages along it—even fairly distant ones—became part of your legal area of operation.

On the other hand, truckload (TL) carriers (also known as consolidated long-route carriers) were licensed not according to the routes they traveled, but according to administrative districts within the prefectures where they operated. The problem was that a TL truck was forbidden to carry mixed loads of freight from multiple clients. However, with permission from the Minister of Transport, you could receive a license permitting you to combine shipments from multiple jurisdictions. So Yamato set about getting licenses as a TL carrier in every prefecture in Japan, and the license to combine shipments.

To a certain extent I could understand requiring a license to engage in freight collection, but this made no sense at all with regard to delivery. After all, we had to transport and deliver the parcels we had collected, whether we had a license or not. So what we normally did for parcels addressed to areas for which we were not licensed was to have them delivered for us by another carrier with whom we had signed a forwarding agreement.

The other thing we thought about was the use of minivans. Trucks were classed as small, medium, and large on the basis of their cargo capacity. But minivans were outside this classification system, had less stringent garaging and inspection regulations, and could be exempted from freight transport licensing with the permission of the prefectural governor. But since they were defined as vehicles having a cargo capacity of less than six hundred kilograms, their operational efficiency was quite poor.

Faced with all this, these were the methods Yamato used in order to expand the sphere of its Takkyūbin operations:

1. We would establish the widest possible collection and delivery zones along the national highways for which we possessed route licenses.
2. We would use our license to combine shipments from multiple jurisdictions to expand operations throughout every prefecture for which we had local licenses.
3. In jurisdictions where we did not have route licenses we would use freight forwarders for transport on the main highways, and for collection and delivery we would secure permission to operate minivans.

Working in this way, we gradually expanded our area of operations, but there were limits to what we could accomplish. So we decided on the one hand to press ahead with applications for licenses, while on the other we worked to buy up operating rights from other businesses in the industry.

Between 1982 and 1985, we were able to buy operating rights to the following routes: Osaka to all of Kyūshū, Hiroshima to the San'in region, Kanazawa to Nanao, Akita to Ōdate, and Osaka to Maizuru. But there were still important major routes for which we could not acquire route licenses. So we had to pursue applications for these licenses—the only legitimate option open to us.

For example, we had a license for the route from Tokyo to Sendai, but not for the routes from Sendai onward to Iwate or Aomori, which meant that we could not extend our area of operations into the northern Tōhoku region. For this we would have to pursue the orthodox approach of applying for a route license.

So in November 1981 we filed an application for an extension of our route license from Sendai to Aomori. But a competitor of ours in Aomori mounted a campaign opposing us, and the application was shelved.

According to the Road Transportation Law, licenses were supposed to be issued on the basis of supply and demand for transport capacity. However, since the Ministry of Transport had no data whatsoever that would allow it to gauge this supply and demand, the reality of the situation was that licenses were issued more or less on the whim of the supervising official. Generally speaking, the thinking behind the decisions was pretty odd: opposition by an established operator was seen as a sign that supply was greater than demand; absence of opposition was seen as indicating the opposite. A ministry official even said quite openly, "We'll be happy to give you a license just as soon as the established operator withdraws his objection."

This was more than I could take. If this was how they worked, what in the world was the point of having a Ministry of Transport at all?

In December 1985, four years after the original application, we filed a formal complaint of nonfeasance with the Minister of Transport under the provisions of the Administrative Appeal Law. Why did we wait four years to file? Because with the Ministry of Transport, it was normal for it to take three years to process an application.

I had no illusions as to what the results would be of protesting to the Minister of Transport regarding what his ministry was up to; the answer was, or course, that the law had not been violated. But it was necessary to go through this formal process if I wanted to take them to court later on.

At last the time was ripe. On August 28, 1986, I filed a lawsuit against the Minister of Transport appealing for recognition of unlawful nonfeasance. The Ministry of Transport was nonplussed by this resort to administrative litigation against a regulatory agency—they were going to have a pretty hard time explaining in court why they had ignored our application for a route license for nearly five years.

According to Ministry of Transport records, in 1985 there were 144 applications for trucking route licenses. They were disposed of as follows: 90 approved, none rejected, 78 withdrawn. What do these figures mean? Well, the Ministry of Transport has not supplied any documentation on which to base an objective explanation of its judgements, so all we know for certain is that none were rejected and 78 were withdrawn. The reason the total of approved and withdrawn applications is larger than the total number of applications for the year is that there were a large number of applications that had not been acted upon for years. I could scarcely contain my anger at the irresponsibility of an agency that would sit on applications for five and six years or more until the applicants finally backed down and withdrew them.

The Ministry of Transport convened a public hearing on our case on October 23, 1986, and on December 2 issued us our license.

From filing to receipt of the license, five long years had passed.

The same thing happened in Kyūshū. On December 25, 1980, we applied for a license to operate on National Highway 3 from Fukuoka via Kumamoto to Kagoshima. Since we made it clear that we would fight for our license there with administrative litigation concurrent with our suit in the Tōhoku case, the ministry held a public hearing in December 1986, and issued us the Kyūshū license in January 1987. In this case it had taken us six years to get our license.

The Ministry of Transport was totally unable to comprehend the difference between commercial freight and consumer parcel service. They apparently could not understand, no matter how many times it was explained to them, that because we were operating in a completely different market, we would not be competing at all with existing commercial freight operators.

Yamato Transport was staking its future as a company on the nationwide expansion of Takkyūbin. I still get angry when I think that in spite of this, Ministry of Transport officials were lording it over us, telling us we could have a license anytime we wanted if we could silence the opposition of established operators.

There are people who have said to me, "You were a pretty cool customer, clashing with the bureaucrats like that." But I didn't especially feel like I was clashing with them. I was just doing what I thought was right. If anything, they were clashing with us. I didn't feel I was doing anything unusual by appealing to the courts for justice in a case in which we had clearly been wronged.

Luckily, Yamato Transport did not go under. But thanks to the bureaucrats, our nationwide expansion was delayed by at least five years. I am still amazed at the thickheadedness of the Ministry of Transport bureaucrats who could not even acknowledge the fact that established institutions are always a bit behind the times, but what I really couldn't bear was their heartlessness in letting applications like ours sit on a shelf for five or six years. The ethics of any occupation are that you do the best job you can with the work that is given to you. We are better off without institutions like the Ministry of Transport that are devoid of any sense of ethics.

In September 1989 we received a license for five routes reaching all of Hokkaidō, adding 1,268 kilometers to our route system. In December of the same year we commenced Takkyūbin service to Ōshima, the largest island in the Izu group, and to Amami Ōshima, the largest of the Amami islands off southern Kyūshū. As a result, at the completion of our third Frontrunner's Three-Year Plan in March 1990, we had succeeded in extending our service area to cover 99.5 percent of Japan's physical area and 99.9 percent of its population.

A Model Change, and Another Battle with the Ministry of Transport

In the beginning, Takkyūbin handled two sizes of parcels: S (up to ten kilograms) and M (up to twenty kilograms), with the shipping charge for the former set ¥100 lower than the latter. It occurred to me that if we added another size smaller than S and at an even cheaper rate, the customers would be happy and it would probably improve sales. Specifically, the idea was to create a P size (up to two kilograms) and charge ¥200 less than for the S, while at the same time raising the price of the M size by ¥100 to make a ¥200 difference between it and the S size as well. The discount at the bottom would balance out the rise at the top.

When we proposed this to the Ministry of Transport, however, the answer was no. The ministry was totally unable to grasp the fact that Takkyūbin and LTL (less-than-load) trucks hauling commercial freight were two completely different types of business, and insisted on treating them as exactly the same. This meant that they were intent on applying the ministry-approved rate schedule for commercial freight to Takkyūbin as well.

The minimum weight on the rate schedule for LTL trucks was thirty kilograms; parcels weighing less than this all had to be charged at the same rate. In point of fact there was a ¥100 difference between what we were charging for our S and M parcels, but since a 20 percent variance above or below the approved rate was tolerated, we were well within the framework of the law. But now we were proposing to create a three-tier price structure, with ¥200 price increases between the P, S, and M classes—in other words, a price structure unique to Takkyūbin and different from the system applied to LTL trucking.

But the Ministry of Transport would not approve this. We tried delivering our new rate schedule to them, but they would not take receipt of the document. When I said, "Then just leave it on the clerk's desk," my staffers told me that the clerks would look over the documents and would only stamp Received on the ones that met with their approval; other documents would not be stamped and would therefore not be regarded as having been received by the ministry.

This was a pretty strange state of affairs. Normally it is the entrepreneur—in this case Yamato Transport—who sets and collects his fees from the client. The Ministry of Transport is there only to monitor whether there is any malfeasance—it should not have the authority to be telling the entrepreneur how to run his business. When I thought of the officious arrogance and contempt for the common man contained in this refusal to accept a separate rate schedule for Takkyūbin, it threw fuel on the flames of my anger.

At the time it was customary for the Ministry of Transport to revise the common rate schedules for various classes of transport every two years. It happened that just as we were trying to establish the new rate schedule for Takkyūbin, the time had come to revise the rate schedule for LTL trucks, and the Ministry of Transport and the Trucking Association were concluding their negotiations.

This was also pretty peculiar, since the Anti-Monopoly Law should have prevented the Trucking Association from acting as representative of the individual companies involved in the industry in discussions with the Ministry of Transport. But the ministry ignored the existence of the individual entrepreneurs, and colluded with the Trucking Association—while of course upholding a facade of formal adherence to the Anti-Monopoly Law. This was how it was done. The Trucking Association had the LTL trucking companies submit only the cover sheets of their applications for rate increases, stamped with the official company seals. The association then took these and stapled them to five different rate schedules it had prepared in advance, and submitted these to the Ministry of Transport. The ministry then appraised these submissions and unified them into a common rate sheet that had already been agreed upon in private consultations with the association. Thus it appeared as if the LTL trucking companies had all submitted individual applications for rate increases—when in fact we had no idea of the contents of our applications.

This time around, however, Yamato Transport refused to submit the cover sheet for its application. Since the refusal of one of the major companies to participate would throw off the whole process, the Ministry of Transport backed down, indicating through the Trucking Association that it was willing to accept our proposal of a compromise by which an application for a special rate schedule for Takkyūbin would be accepted if Yamato would go ahead and submit the LTL trucking application. So we submitted both.

The Takkyūbin application was finally accepted by the ministry— which then proceeded to sit on it for an entire year. We then initiated the next phase of our strategy—an appeal through the mass media. If we were going to fight it out with the ministry of Transport, we were not going to gain any support by keeping the battle behind closed doors. I had always felt our best bet in taking on the ministry was getting public opinion on our side.

So once again, in March 1983, we applied for approval of a new rate schedule that divided our Takkyūbin rates into three classes based on size.

We also named June 1 as the date on which the new rates would go into effect—an unusual move. Up to this time, the Ministry of Transport had unilaterally determined the implementation date for new rate schedules at the time they were approved. I had a hard time swallowing this—it seemed to me that the timing of rate changes ought to be up to the entrepreneur. So when I submitted the application in March, I informed the ministry that we intended to implement the new rates in June, and requested that they consider the application accordingly.

Meanwhile, we placed banner ads on the front page of all the major dailies announcing our new P size and its ¥200 cheaper rate, and informing the public it would be available June 1.

The Ministry of Transport completely ignored our application. So on the front page of the morning editions of May 31 we ran another set of banner ads—saying that because the Ministry of Transport had still not approved it, we were forced to delay the introduction of the P size we had scheduled for June 1.

I am told this enraged ministry officials. But public opinion—supported by the fact that both the Administrative Management Agency and the Second Ad Hoc Commission on Administrative Reform had recommended a revision in the rates for Takkyūbin—was critical of the ministry's foot-dragging. In any event, on July 6 the ministry approved our application.

Bureaucrats in general—not just Ministry of Transport officials—seem to have an innate and deep-seated fear of appearing in print. As a result, newspapers, radio, and television are extremely effective media for exposing the misdeeds of the bureaucracy. But in order to do this you must also be sure that the mass media have a correct understanding of your position. That was why I resorted to newspaper ads.

There is a tendency for popular opinion to shrug its shoulders and accept what the government has to say, even if what it says is wrong or doesn't make sense. This attitude on the part of the people invites a bad attitude on the part of officials—something that we, the people, should reflect upon.

The Myth That Doing Business in Underpopulated Areas Loses Money

Our three Frontrunner's Three-Year Plans had expanded the Takkyūbin network throughout the country. But within the company there was initially a great deal of opposition to the idea of extending our operations into remote and underpopulated areas, out of fear for what this would do to our profitability.

Expanding our area of operations by acquiring route licenses through-out the country did not necessarily mean taking our business into sparsely populated areas. Even in the more remote prefectures there is a distinction between urban and rural areas. We could have chosen to operate only in regional cities and not in their rural hinterlands. As a private company, that might have even been the more likely choice—we were under no obligation to risk losses by providing service to rural areas. Couldn't we leave that job to the postal service? There was a certain logic to the idea that service to such unprofitable areas was the responsibility of the government, not us.

When I first decided to go ahead with Takkyūbin, it was a leap of faith. Luckily, the gamble paid off, and after five years we had reached our initial goals. But the next step—extending our service to the hinterland—required another leap of faith. If, having finally achieved profitability, we wrecked it by working in the boondocks, what was the point?

But the more I thought about it, the more I began to question the formula that rural areas were synonymous with underpopulation, and underpopulation synonymous with losing money.

In big cities housing is concentrated. In rural areas, it is much more dispersed, which means your collection and delivery distances are going to be greater for the same number of packages. But most of the roads are paved. In Gunma or Shimane or other prefectures, the ratio of car ownership is greater than in the big cities, since public transportation is not as developed. Rural roads are good, and have fewer stoplights; in big cities you would be lucky to do twenty kilometers an hour, while in less populated regions you might do forty, cutting your travel time in half. If you think about it in this way, it might not necessarily be true that pickup and delivery is less efficient in these areas than in the cities, or that costs are higher as a result.

Since there would be fewer competitors in the hinterland, Takkyūbin would enjoy a higher rate of use, so our facilities and delivery vans would probably be kept busy.

Japan is a mountainous country, and there is no denying the fact that in the hinterland there are many isolated communities scattered among the mountains. But there would be few packages going to and from these remote villages to other equally remote villages. Packages from these isolated areas would mostly be bound for the major urban areas, and the packages they were receiving would largely come from the cities. Collection and delivery in remote areas might be costly, but packages bound to and from them would increase the volume of parcels carried by urban collection and delivery vans, thus increasing their operating ratio and reducing their costs. In short, there was really no reason to think that expanding our operations into these remote communities would have a significant negative impact on profitability.

Extending our service not just to the prefectures but to their smallest rural communities as well made it possible for us to claim quite truthfully that we would go anywhere in Japan our customers needed us. This gave us a real competitive edge, and was enormously effective in promoting our sales.

Participatory Management

Participatory management means making a clear presentation of the goals and objectives of management, and then stepping back to let the employees themselves take responsibility for the execution of their jobs without detailed directions from the top regarding how the work should be done. In this chapter I will discuss the human resources and labor management aspects of the participatory management system I introduced at the time we launched Takkyūbin.

The standard-bearers of Takkyūbin are some thirty-thousand "sales drivers" (SDs) who have direct contact with our customers in the field. They have to handle a variety of tasks well: collection and delivery of parcels, sales, collection of fees. The job requires the sort of versatility and skill you see in a master sushi chef. They are like the forwards in soccer—and how to keep them motivated and enjoying their work is the crucial question. The success of participatory management depends upon it.

Respecting the abilities of these front-line workers, I have done away with the outmoded seniority system. This was essential to the success of participatory management, but the biggest key is communication within the company.

An Organization with Self-Starters on the Front Lines

When we were involved in commercial freight, the nucleus of our sales efforts was the sales managers at each of our branch offices.

These sales managers would establish connections with their opposite numbers in the shipping departments of potential clients and work out shipping contracts with them, after which we could be assured of a steady stream of daily orders. As long as the sales managers did not neglect the maintenance of these connections—wining and dining the clients, playing golf with them from time to time—a steady revenue stream was more or less assured.

When the sales manager got an order from one of these clients, a driver would be sent to pick up the shipment from the shipping clerks at the client's factory or warehouse. It was a daily operation, requiring little thought and posing no problems.

But with Takkyūbin this way of doing business was impossible. After all, the clients were the general public—mainly housewives. The customers changed every day, as did their locations. No information about shipments was available in advance.

I mulled this over, and concluded that the only way to handle this was to have our front-line drivers serve as the antennae for information regarding shipments. So when we started Takkyūbin, I decided to create a system at Yamato Transport in which the drivers became the backbone of both our sales and operations—a concept I tried to make clear by giving them all the title of "sales drivers," frequently abbreviated to "SD."

As I mentioned in chapter 2, I had been thinking for some time about how to create a new personnel management system embodying the ideal of participatory management, spurred by Sophia University professor Shinoda Yūjirō's concept of "managerial partnership." Now, with the launch of Takkyūbin, I decided to push ahead with restructuring our personnel and labor management system in line with a participatory management model.

Participatory management means that all employees are working toward the same managerial objectives and share the same set of goals, but that each employee thinks for himself in terms of the methods by which these goals are to be achieved—in other words, it is predicated on the autonomous activity of the employees. Management sets goals for the employees, but does not give them orders or instructions regarding how the work is to be done, so that each employee takes responsibility for his own performance.

Some people might wonder whether this is really feasible—but with Takkyūbin, there was no other way to do it.

According to Professor Shinoda, "There are many examples of managerial partnership, and many successful examples of it. It is an easy concept for Japanese to understand, and one for which they are well-suited." And in fact, when I tried implementing it, I found it was an arrangement that gave employees a greater sense of satisfaction and pride in their work.

When we first launched Takkyūbin, I was frequently asked what made it different from the postal service's small parcel service. True, both were large-scale operations involving a division of labor between collection and delivery, sorting by destination, and transport operations. But the Yamato employees handling Takkyūbin have a clear sense of their mission and take personal responsibility for carrying it out. That is the difference, I think.

For instance, an employee collecting parcels in Aomori is conscious of the fact that his work is essential to the delivery of those parcels in other cities. As he does his work, he is thinking of what time he must finish the collection in order to see that the parcels are loaded onto the trucks departing for Sendai, or Tokyo, or Osaka. The attitude is not one of responsibility for only a part of a process: "Oh, I've finished the collections, so my job is done." It is working with a sense of responsibility for making sure that those parcels can be delivered the next day, without fail, to their destinations. It is like the members of a relay race team, each doing his utmost to ensure the team's victory. And the results of this may be seen in the difference in level of service between Takkyūbin and the postal service.

In the field, the SDs responsible for collection and delivery form groups. Each group has a leader, rotated on a regular basis, to coordinate its activities and train new members of the team. Each SD has his own area of operations, and has created his own operations manual, consisting of a map of the area and notes regarding his route: dangerous intersections, regularly scheduled pickups, and so forth. The SDs decide where Takkyūbin agents are needed, and encourage them to sign contracts with us. Development of new customers is also their responsibility.

In the centers and depots, wall charts display the objectives and the performance of each SD. Participatory management means taking one's autonomy seriously and being responsible for one's performance. Base salaries are supplemented by performance-based bonuses, but there is no thought of commissions or the like. In the future, I would like to see us move in the direction of a profit-sharing system.

Responsibility for monitoring working hours belongs to the manager of each center, and he checks to make sure that each of the employees under him is working the appropriate number of hours each month and getting the appropriate number of days off.

The spirit of participatory management is the company's corporate culture. Our SDs are often praised by our customers for their friendliness and helpfulness. Of course we do what we can to train our employees, but I think this comes more from the fact that they have taken Yamato's corporate culture to heart, and decide what to do and how to do it by putting themselves in the customer's shoes.

In Japan, the basic regulations concerning management of workers are contained in the Labor Standards Law. But one of the things I have constantly wondered about during my time as an employer is why the law makes an issue only of the length of working hours, and not the quality or intensity of the work.

Overtime—lots of it—is characteristic of Japanese companies. And since Japanese working hours are longer than those of other countries, we are told we must shorten them. However, for the workers, what overtime means is that they get paid more for doing the same work slowly than if they did it quickly. Overtime is the most expedient way for them to increase their income. Employers have thus come up with various ways to try to limit overtime pay, but there is always a question of whether these will run afoul of the formalities of the Labor Standards Law. I think this is a problem with the law itself.

In the transport industry, once drivers have left the depot, they work without supervision. For example, when they are hauling freight between Tokyo and Osaka their official working hours run from the time of departure to the time of arrival; nobody but the driver knows what happened in-between. If they are later than usual, the managers have no way of knowing—other than the driver's own word—whether the driver was stuck in a traffic jam or taking a nap at a drive-in.

The law requires a tachometer on all long-distance trucks. If we suppose that ten trucks a day make the run from Tokyo to Osaka, then in a year's time we could accumulate a database of 3,650 tachograms recording their travel times. There would be no practical problem in using this as a basis on which labor and management could work out an agreement for standard travel times of, say, 70 kilometers an hour on freeways and 40 kilometers an hour on regular roads.

However, the regulatory agency says it cannot approve this system because, strictly speaking, exceptions to these standard travel times would then constitute a violation of the Labor Standards Law. What a perfectly bureaucratic way of thinking about this!

Computation of working hours is the basis for paying fair wages, and requires objective and accurate calculation. However, I can't help but question the fairness of a formalistic application of the present Labor Standards Law, which considers only the length of working hours and not the quality or intensity of the work.

To achieve fairness, there must be a relationship of trust between labor and management. The participatory management system, in which workers do their work autonomously, without orders or instructions, is premised upon such trust. We are accustomed to thinking of participatory management in terms of tertiary industries, but I believe it is also quite applicable to secondary industries.

The Sales Driver as Sushi Chef

I have always told Yamato's sales drivers that I want them to be like sushi chefs.

When you go to a sushi restaurant, you have to decide whether you want to sit at the counter or at a table. If you sit at a table, you have your choice of set menus—usually named Pine, Bamboo, and Plum—clearly graded according to both content and price. No worry about what you are going to have to pay at the end. On the other hand, when you sit at the counter you can chat with the chef, choose your favorite types of sushi à la carte, and have him prepare them for you—but you have to be prepared to spend a bit more money than if you were sitting at a table. Most people don't go out to eat sushi that often, and many feel that sitting at the counter is the most fun.

The sushi chef goes early in the morning to buy his fish, and prepares each type in the manner appropriate to it. He lets customers know what is especially good that day, and takes their orders. He puts customers at their ease by chatting with them about this and that. He gives a bit of a sales pitch, telling customers which fish are in season, and so forth, and takes more orders. When customers are getting full, he might recommend a light hand-roll such as pickled plum to end their meal. When they ask for the check, he tells them how much they owe. A sushi shop gains popularity because of the spirit of the man behind the counter; a shop with a chef who knows how to work the counter is a shop people will want to come back to.

Before Takkyūbin, when we were dealing in commercial freight, the way we operated was more like the cafeterias in the big department stores, where there is a clear division of labor between the cashiers, the cooks for Japanese, Western, and Chinese food, the waiters and waitresses, and the busboys.

When we started Takkyūbin, I declared that we were going to shift from this cafeteria style of doing business to the sushi-shop style, and I asked the sales drivers to see themselves as sushi chefs. In other words, they were going to have to become skilled at a variety of on-the-job tasks—finding the customers, writing the waybills, carrying the parcels, logging everything into the computer system, collecting the money, answering customers' questions, and so on.

Working one-on-one with any and all customers—that is the core of the SDs' job. Yet in the beginning, our veteran drivers balked at this: "We joined Yamato because we like to drive trucks. This computer stuff is for secretaries. And don't even talk to us about collecting money. If we lose any of it we're going to have to pay out of pocket, I bet. No thanks."

I hadn't anticipated such a reaction.

So I assigned a lot of our newer employees to be sales drivers. People with some experience as warehouse clerks were well-suited to the job. On the other hand, people with experience as drivers for other trucking companies usually refused. They generally had no desire to do anything other than driving, and most of them had little understanding of the concept of participatory management. On the other hand, former warehouse clerks were perfectly comfortable with the idea of multitasking—taking orders, receiving goods, driving, collecting money—and took up their new jobs as sales drivers with little or no resistance.

Yet even Yamato's veteran drivers who complained in the beginning were gradually won over when they went on deliveries and were actually thanked by the customers. This was something they had never experienced in all their years of delivering commercial freight. They were surprised— and touched. And motivated.

As older employees did the work of sales drivers, they got used to the tasks other than driving that the job required. And they all began to realize that compared with the strict division of labor that had prevailed before, their new jobs were more interesting and meaningful because they could master a variety of tasks and see a job through from beginning to end. Taking such responsibility for their work was a challenge, but one that was rewarded with a sense of purpose and accomplishment.

There are many business types in the food industry. Department-store cafeterias, restaurants in train stations and airports, *gyūdon* chains, gourmet Japanese restaurants, Korean barbecue houses, hamburger franchises, and so forth. Each has its own characteristics. But I felt that among all of them, the sushi shop was what had the most in common with Takkyūbin.

A sushi shop has to have the proper facilities for preparing the food. It has to have an appealing atmosphere. But more important than anything else is the personality of the chef—the man behind the counter making the food. An honest and straightforward character—not insincere flattery —is what wins customer's trust. And of course he must also have an excellent knowledge of fish, and skill in its preparation.

Takkyūbin's sales drivers naturally need to be good drivers. But if that's all they can do, it's a problem. The job also demands a knowledge of the geography of all of Japan. But more than anything, it requires sincerity and honesty and the ability to see things from the customers' perspective.

In a sushi shop the owner and his wife are in the supporting roles. The real star must be the chef. With Takkyūbin as well, the depot or center manager and the team leaders are also supporting parts. It is the SD who must be the star. To me this is the core of the comparison.

Be Star Forwards!

While I told the SDs that I wanted them to be like popular sushi chefs, I also asked them to be like talented soccer forwards.

Soccer is currently enjoying quite a boom in Japan, and the fans can get awfully passionate in their support for their favorite teams. What really seems to get them going is the phenomenal skill of the star players.

Soccer requires teamwork, and there are no victories without tightly coordinated play on the part of all the team's members. Yet in the final analysis, what scores points is talented forwards who can seize exactly the right moment to make their shot at the goal. Skill alone does not make a star player. The ability to make instantaneous judgments on whether to pass or try to score—and act on them instantaneously—is essential. SDs also need, when a customer makes a special request, to be able to make an immediate judgment as to how to handle it. They don't have time to put in a call to the center to get instructions from the manager. When there are complaints, they also must know how to handle them appropriately and immediately.

More than anything else they need to be able to think and act on their own in terms of seeking out and negotiating new business. Takkyūbin is like collecting water from an underground stream, drop by drop, and it all begins with the work of our front-line personnel—the SDs. So I would often say something like this when I spoke with them:

"At Yamato Transport, the president and the execs don't bring in a single yen. Our only way to get revenue is by the SDs collecting parcels from the customers, one parcel at a time. In other words, if the SDs, who are the forwards on our team, don't make a shot, we don't score any goals. To make an effective shot at the goal you've got to have an accurate pass from your buddies in the backfield. If you are reliable and conscientious in delivering the parcels that your buddies have collected from all over the country, then there is a good chance we will get more business from the people who sent them. I am well aware of the fact that it is your judgment and your actions that will bring increased income to the company, and I want you to be star forwards."

I also changed the way our organization charts were drawn. Back in the days when we were handling commercial freight, the branch managers were at the top, followed by the sales managers and sales reps, while the drivers were all lumped together at the very bottom of the chart. So I reversed the chart to look like the roster of a soccer team, with the SDs or forwards at the top, and the branch manager, or goalie, at the bottom. I wanted the SDs to realize they were the key players on our team.

Forwards are needed for more than offense. When the ball passes to the opponent, they have to play defense as well. If they discover when they are making their deliveries that a package has been damaged, they must immediately apologize to the customer and take appropriate action. In the early days of Takkyūbin, our manual instructed the SDs to immediately report any unusual occurrences to their branch manager and get instructions from him.

But soon Takkyūbin got on track and the volume of parcels we were handling grew explosively. Problem parcels were a tiny percentage of the whole, but their numbers rose with the expansion of our overall volume of freight. At that point I expanded the authorization given to the drivers to resolve cases of damage, and allowed them to pay out as much as ¥300,000 per incident on their own discretion.

Up to that point, if a parcel had been damaged, the SD had to report this to the center manager, who would then offer apologies and investigate the appropriate amount of payment for damages. In other words, he would ask the customer for an estimate of the value of the damaged item. The center manager of course wanted to keep the damage payment to a minimum, and after negotiating on this basis with the customer, a sum would be settled on. Then the center manager would report this to his superior, the branch manager, and ask for his approval. The whole process was time-consuming—three weeks or a month could go by for no good reason. Meanwhile, even if the customers had accepted the fact of the accident itself, they would no doubt be angered by the amount of time it was taking to resolve the issue.

When I expanded the amount the SDs were authorized to pay out to ¥300,000, I gave the following instructions to them and to the center managers: "From now on, if an accident occurs, I want the driver to go to the customer the next day with cash and an apology, and resolve the matter on the spot. If we do that, even if we can't do anything about the accident, at least the customer will see we are doing our best to resolve the issue, and will probably forgive us. And it should also decrease the amount of damages. . . ."

At first my last comment appears to have been misunderstood, for a number of managers replied that if more time were given to negotiating the payments, they could probably be reduced. So I explained myself further. If we simply accepted the amount the customer named and had the driver pay it the following day, the amount of damages we were paying would end with the value of the item in question. If the center manager spent a month negotiating the damages, it would wind up being the value of the item plus the amount of the center manager's salary and the branch manager's salary corresponding to the time spent on the issue. In the long run it would be a lot cheaper to just have the drivers pay damages to the customer the next day.

Talented athletes are also good at recovering from their errors. I wanted the SDs to be star players adept at all facets of the game—passing, scoring, and recovering the ball—and in fact they fulfilled the hopes I had for them.

America is Pro Baseball, Japan is High School Baseball

Human resources setups in Japan and the United States are at opposite ends of the spectrum.

First off, consider hiring. In America, a company advertises the skills it is looking for, offers a salary and benefits package to people that meet them, and once agreement is reached, signs a contract. If an employee does not demonstrate the skills specified in the contract, the contract is terminated. The contract is the basis of the entire relationship.

In Japan, on the other hand, the concept of the contract has been almost nonexistent. When new college grads are hired, such things as skills and contracts are not mentioned. Of course selections are made from amid the pool of new graduates, but requirements for specific skills are not stated. Nor do the students themselves work to acquire specific competencies while in school—such as in marketing or information systems—that companies might be looking for. The corporation looks at the overall character and personality of the students, their potential for development, and especially whether they are likely to fit in with the corporate culture, and makes its decision. Training in necessary skills and competencies will take place after the individual has joined the company.

If the American way of buying skills with contracts is pro baseball, then the Japanese way is high school baseball. When the new freshmen arrive each April at the beginning of the new school year, the various athletic teams compete to sign up the biggest and strongest-looking among them, regardless of prior experience. Once they've joined the team, the older students show them the ropes. Of course not all of them will make it onto the diamond, but none of them will be cut from the team for incompetence, either. If they want, they can remain a member of the team until they graduate.

When the hiring season comes around, a corporate interviewer will ask the student if he was active in sports. If he says, "Yes, I was on the baseball team," the interviewer will ask, "Well, how did you do?"

"Not so well. We usually got eliminated in the first round of the prefectural games."

"How did you do personally?"

"I didn't even make second string, and spent all my time chasing balls in practice. But I got a chance to be part of the baseball team, and it was an experience I'll remember all my life when I look back on my youth."

For sports activity in school, this may be fine. At least he seems to have had a good time. But from the point of view of a potential employer, this is not so good.

The individual may be satisfied even if he doesn't become a starting player (executive) and may lead a contented existence until graduation (retirement), but if everybody had this kind of attitude, the team (company) would keep getting beat in the preliminary rounds.

At this point, someone might say, why not introduce a meritocratic system? But you can't do that in Japan. Why? Because you can't force an incompetent employee to resign. First of all, because the competencies required of the individual were never defined. Work is organized as the work of a group.

There are advantages and disadvantages to everything. This group orientation may be unsuited to the development of individual skills, but it has the merit of inspiring greater loyalty to the company. And as the changing times demand new skills from the work force, in-house training eases transitions in job description and work routines.

It has become a terribly competitive world, and Japanese companies can no longer continue their high-school baseball approach to human resources management. At the same time, there can be no success in rushing to adopt the American contract-based system. Japanese and American corporate cultures are too different to allow this.

I think we have no choice but to try to preserve the strong points of a management system grounded in Japanese culture, while trying to eliminate its deficiencies. You can't build a baseball team entirely out of starting players. You also need your second-string, and your ball-chasers and groundskeepers. If all of them band together with the common goal of winning the pennant, and really put their hearts into daily practice, then victory is possible. I think it should be one goal of corporate management to make it possible for the ball-chasers and groundskeepers to "graduate" with pride and with no regrets for how they have spent their lives, as long as they have carried out their duties to the best of their abilities.

On the other hand, you don't want to have so many team members that they get in each others' way during practice. Paying attention to always maintaining the appropriate number of players is the role of the manager.

The biggest drawback to group-oriented management is the seniority system. If incompetent senior team members try to boss the regular players around, the team is not going to win. In Japan, a large number of firms have adopted an escalator-style system of automatic promotions, and this is a terrible mistake. A winning team is a team in which the senior players really lead their juniors, take the initiative in helping care for the grounds and picking up the practice balls, and by so doing unite the spirit of the entire team. We need to come up with a human resources management system that encourages this kind of thoroughgoing behind-the-scenes work on the part of the senior players.

The adoption of a salary system based on annual contracts is being advocated. I don't think it's a bad idea. But as I have said before, Japanese companies are not the big leagues. They're high school baseball. The sun cannot shine only on the starting players—we must also find ways to make the ball-chasers and groundskeepers and trainers feel they are making a worthwhile contribution.

Specifically, we need to junk the seniority-based system of promotion to executive positions and use a merit-based system to put the right people in the right positions. We should also adopt a system of compensation that is determined by the individual's contribution to the company, regardless of his position. There is a problem with basing evaluations on a superficial reading of the numbers. Someone whose numbers are good may be actually resting on the accomplishments of his predecessor. I think it is more important to bring the element of individual character into evaluations. I think that placing a premium on people of good character will, in the long run, contribute to the development of the company. Isn't it time we came up with a system that really suits Japanese corporate culture?

For Japanese, Work Worth Doing Makes a Life Worth Living

The crucial difference between Japan and the United States lies in attitudes towards work. And I think this comes from different views of life.

For many Americans, work is simply an unavoidable way of making a living, a kind of wage slavery. Of course there are also people whose work is informed by a sense of mission, but I think they are in the minority. Once, on a visit to an American company, I saw everyone head for home on the dot at five o'clock, leaving their work unfinished. They had a clear sense of the amount of time to devote to work on the one hand and their family and home life on the other—and in their preservation of these boundaries I felt I had glimpsed something fundamental in the American way of life. This is clearly expressed in attitudes toward retirement. I've been surprised by hearing Americans a year or two away from retirement chatting happily about how soon they will be able to devote all their time to golf.

How many Japanese salarymen a couple of years away from retirement chat happily about it? I think Japanese for whom retirement is a happy prospect are still definitely in the minority. When a retiring colleague comes around to say his farewells, isn't it more common to thank him for all his hard work than to congratulate him on his retirement?

For working people, days off are a happy thing. Now that the two-day weekend has finally established itself in Japan, we all have a chance to rest and relax. But is anyone really happy with retirement, when every day is a day off? No matter how good a pension you are collecting, I doubt a life that consists only of holidays is really all that much fun.

For Japanese, work is what gives their life meaning. In Japan as well, I suppose there are people who are working at jobs they dislike simply to earn an income. And I imagine in such cases work feels like slavery. But for the majority of Japanese, I believe that work is something that makes them feel life is worth living.

A strong sense of identification with their company and a strong sense of engagement in their work is characteristic of Japanese people. Why else would they stop off on the way home from work to hoist a few drinks at a neighborhood bar and grouse about their bosses? If they really hated their company and their supervisors, they could simply go home and forget about it. I don't think they get together to bitch at the local bar because they hate their work—quite the contrary. I think they criticize their company over drinks because they really love it.

"If I were president of the company, this is what I would do"; "if I were the section chief I'd do things differently"—it seems to me that such criticism of company officers and supervisors arises out of the fact that the employee always thinks of himself as a member of the company and a participant in its affairs. These bull sessions over drinks are actually evidence of affection for the company, and I think they show a healthy attitude. It's a question of whether these remarks are taking place in an informal or a formal situation. Every employee has opinions about the company, which tend to be expressed more critically in an informal setting, and more constructively in a formal one. In any event, this almost innate sense of participation in the company shared by most Japanese is something that managers should always work to encourage.

Participation in management gives employees a sense that their work is worth doing. And worthwhile work, for a Japanese, means a worthwhile life. This is something that gives employees a happiness that is completely distinct from monetary concerns.

Building a Motivated Team

A company full of motivated employees and one full of slackers are going to produce totally different results. But what can you do to motivate your employees? This is one of the biggest questions facing a manager.

First of all, you need to think about situations in which it is hard to get motivated. You are given a job. You are assigned goals. You are told in exhaustive detail how you must perform the job. And you are not allowed to make any changes, even if you think there is a better way of doing it. Not exactly a recipe for enthusiasm, is it?

If the goals of management are explained by the top executives, and the employees are told that the way they are being instructed to do things is best from the point of view of integration with the work of all the other employees, they will probably be persuaded. But if no such explanations are given, and they are forbidden by their superiors from altering procedures even when see a better way to do their job, they will probably feel frustrated and apathetic.

Japan has very high educational standards. Not only white-collar employees, but many blue-collar workers as well, have had some higher education. Their sense of belonging to the company is strong, as is their loyalty to it. With people like this, it is not necessary to micromanage their work. In fact, if you try to, it will probably backfire on you. Nobody really likes being micromanaged; it feels a lot better to be trusted to operate independently. This is true of blue-collar workers too, and in many cases, it is blue-collar work that gets done the most effectively if you leave the workers alone and let them do their job.

So how do you motivate employees, have them perform their work with self-direction and self-discipline, and achieve the desired results? The key word is communication. Specifically, corporate goals must be clearly expressed and clear objectives defined. Time constraints must be explained. The situation with regard to competing firms should be described. The company's strategic plan should be outlined. When this has been done, everyone should be asked to think about tactics: the specific ways to accomplish these goals. And they should understand why they are being asked to do this.

Unfortunately, the larger the organization, the more likely it is that there will be people within the organization acting as spoilers of morale. This is something you have to keep a careful eye on. These are frequently middle managers and supervisors, and it is the old-timers you have to watch most carefully.

Employees like this tend to want to micromanage the work of their subordinates based on their own work experience, while at the same time not being very good at explaining the whys and wherefores of company policy and planning. This can be the juncture at which communication within the company is short-circuited. Yet precisely because of this, middle management can play a crucial part in promoting communication. Never forget that whether or not these middle managers are doing their job properly can be the factor determining whether or not you can build a team of motivated employees.

The rank-and-file employees may be fired up to do their work, but between them and company president there are several layers of managers, and this is where obstacles to clear communication can arise. A communication system is functioning well when information is transmitted accurately from person to person—but achieving this accurate transmission is in fact extremely difficult. People process what they hear selectively, and that is what they transmit to the next person. In the process, the information can frequently become garbled. So it is best to have as few layers of management as possible between the president and the front-line employees.

Still, it is hard for the president to have a direct connection with the front lines. In the case of Yamato Transport, the president has direct contact via a monthly executive conference with the vice-presidents in charge of each regional bloc. Between these vice-presidents and the front-line sales drivers are the branch managers and then the center managers—and it is maintaining accurate lines of communication through these layers that is important.

At the same time, if information is to be correctly transmitted, it must be expressed effectively. You can tell employees to boost sales or raise profits and they will simply shrug it off as so much hot air. This is not effective communication. Communication must be concrete and explicit. Like the slogan "First service, then profits," it must be concise and clear in its intent.

In Japan we have a traditional candy called Kintarō *ame*. It's in the form of a stick, and no matter where you cut it, the face of Kintarō, the golden boy of the fairy tale, appears on the end. A company needs to be like this candy. The design of Kintarō's face cannot be too complex—it is the simplicity and clarity of the design that ensures its appearance wherever you cut the candy. The president of a company must always work to make sure his face and voice are communicated to the employees. And this is true not only within the company, but in terms of the mass media, where he needs to make his existence known. No matter what the circumstances, he must train himself to deliver a concise, consistent message.

The more opportunity there is for direct contact with customers, the easier it is to foster employee morale. In that sense, it is easier to create a participatory management system in tertiary industry than it is in manufacturing. Of course in manufacturing as well, you can also foster employee motivation by giving them the room to exercise their talents and ingenuity. But I think our Takkyūbin operations have proved to be especially fertile ground for the practice of participatory management.

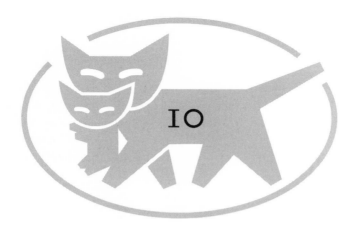

Working with Labor Unions

Yamato Transport's labor union has at times been ahead of the managerial team in proposing new corporate strategy. It was the labor union that suggested we make Takkyūbin a 365-day-a-year service. Why was the labor union proposing something that could be taken as an extension of working hours? Because the SDs in the front lines were trying to respond to customer demand. This was one of the fruits of the participatory management policies I discussed in chapter 9.

In the past, Yamato Transport, like many Japanese companies, had a deeply adversarial relationship with the union. We shifted to a policy of reconciliation when we were launching Takkyūbin. At that point the company and the union realized they needed to work together in order to survive, and gave up pointless squabbling.

Now management and labor work together to improve the conditions of employment—and this way of thinking has become the norm for our company.

The Role of the Union

Every company has a union. Really small ones may not, but for mid-sized companies on up, unions are a fact of life.

Business executives may accept this fact of life, but I imagine the majority, if they spoke frankly, would say that they'd rather not have unions.

There was a time when I thought so myself. That was also a time when the unions were permeated with an ideological approach to the world and refused to engage in honest dialogue. This doctrinaire approach was especially strong in the period right after the war when a union was first organized at Yamato Transport, and union leaders boasted that the workers would survive, even if the company folded.

Every year when the spring labor offensive came around with its demands for wage increases, the company would respond with the best it could do given its financial situation, and the union response would be "How do you expect us to live on these wages!" This really irritated me—since it seemed to me they had enough money to go out drinking every night!

The union leaders at the time were good at stirring up the rank and file, but there were not many of them who were responsible enough to persuade their members to make the necessary compromises when the time had come. As a result, the company almost always ended up being forced to give a bit more in terms of wage hikes than it should have. I'd then be surprised to hear some of the union leaders who had taken the hardest line saying privately, "Can the company really afford it? I think maybe they're giving us too much."

My father always used to say, "Love the employee, but come down hard on the union member." At first I didn't really understand what he meant, since every employee was also a union member. However, over time I experienced an interesting phenomenon: a person who, when thinking of himself as an employee would naturally have the best interests of the company in mind, would then say something completely different when he was operating in his capacity as a union member. This made me appreciate the wisdom of my father's words.

At that time, the union and the company were locked in a relationship of mutual distrust, each side convinced the other was concealing or distorting the truth. So in wage negotiations, for instance, there was a lot of unnecessary pulling and hauling. The company would intentionally make an almost absurdly low first offer, which the union would force up bit by bit in a series of four or five proposals and counterproposals, until the company finally declared as its final offer a sum slightly below what it had anticipated from the beginning, so that the union could make a show of forcing that up one last notch, the company could make a show of grudgingly compromising, and the matter would finally be settled.

I don't know how many times I proposed we put an end to such time-consuming and totally unproductive negotiations. They continued, however, because the union leaders, while acknowledging that they were a waste of time, felt that this ritual was indispensable to satisfying the rank and file, who expected to see protracted negotiations and not the acceptance of an initial offer, even a reasonable one.

Yamato's union was one of the tamer ones, but it seems to have felt it necessary to justify its existence with a strike, so a twenty-four-hour strike was planned for the spring labor offensive of 1961. At first we were able to persuade the union to exempt our operations for our biggest client, Mitsukoshi, but in the end, citing heavy pressure from the rank and file, the union ended up bringing our work for Mitsukoshi to a halt as well.

At the time I was vice-president in charge of our department store operations, and was appalled at the damage this was likely to do to the relationship of trust we had built up with our most important clients. But my father, then president of the company, said "Come with me," and took me to a meeting with Iwase Eiichirō, the president of Mitsukoshi. My father began by apologizing for the trouble the strike would cause, but said that the only way to prevent it was to give the union more money than they deserved, which would probably lead to a hike in Yamato's rates, so the best thing was to let them go ahead and strike. President Iwase was very supportive, telling us to hang tough, and we never heard a word of complaint from him about any inconvenience caused by the strike.

In those days I had a rather critical attitude toward my father, but in this case I was filled with the greatest respect, feeling I had learned a valuable lesson in what it means to be a business leader. And I believe the reason he had ordered me to come along with him was to teach me this lesson.

My father hated compromising with the union, but as a man he was pretty soft-hearted. The union leaders were well aware of this, and the final scene in negotiations was often some sob story or other, at which point my father would throw reason to the winds, cave in, and leave me to deal with the consequences. This used to make me furious, and was one of the sources of my negative attitude towards the union. Yet I now understand that my father, seeing my naive and rigidly logical approach to dealing with the unions, probably wanted to teach me that you can't run a company on logic alone.

The same person will say one thing when speaking as an employee, and something totally different when speaking as a union member. At first this surprised me, but I gradually came to see it as a matter of fact. The rise of the postwar labor movement brought radical improvements in working conditions for the average worker, so it is no surprise that our employees' identification of themselves as union members grew stronger.

There is something else we must not overlook here: one of the functions of the labor union is to provide a check on management.

Just about every company has a joint management council comprised of members from both management and labor. My father didn't like the sound of "joint management" because he thought it encroached on his rights as entrepreneur, so he called it the "joint business promotion council." We still call it that at Yamato, but its role is no different from the joint management councils most people are familiar with.

In the days just prior to launching Takkyūbin, I had already decided to introduce a participatory management system at Yamato Transport. Hearing of this, one of the labor union officials came to me to complain. "You're giving us a lot of sweet talk about participatory management and so on, but I think what you really have up your sleeve is union-busting." I was dumbfounded. "Nothing could be further from my mind. Why are you saying this?" "Can't you see? If all the employees become managers, the union is finished!" I could see he had a point.

But I carefully explained to him that I had no interest in busting the union. In fact, I believe without labor unions management would get nowhere. Why? Because when you are running a company, you can make policies and establish concrete objectives, but you can never really be sure if the entire company, down to the last employee, is getting the message. If you ask the executives, they'll tell you everything's OK. Even if you believe them, there's no way to check. But in meetings with union officials, I have repeatedly heard them say—and found it to be true when I checked up on it, "Management may be talking a good line, but do you know that out in the field a lot of folks are doing something completely different from what we've been instructed to do?"

In other words, top management rarely sees what is going on in the field or on the shop floor, and while they are happy to be the bearers of good news, they never want to bring bad news to the president. As is often said, it is lonely at the top. And it is the labor union that helps in breaking out of that isolation and the problems it causes. I'll put it strongly, because I believe it: without labor unions responsible management is impossible.

If you drink a lot, you're likely to get ulcers. But if you have sharp stomach pains after a night of hard drinking, you're a lot more likely to take it easy that day and cut out the booze. If your stomach didn't bother you at all, no matter how much you drank, you might be less inclined to moderation, and actually develop ulcers. So it's a good thing your tummy hurts when it is out of sorts.

In the healthy management of a company, it is also necessary to feel some pain when things are not going right. And I believe it is the role of the labor union to transmit that pain to management.

When the union complained to me about the participatory management scheme, this was the explanation I offered them, and it seemed to convince them that I was not out to break the union.

How to Avoid "Restructuring"

Labor unions are something no company can do without, but the nature of the unions varies greatly from company to company. Businessmen like it when their company union adopts a conciliatory policy toward management and cooperates with company policy, but things do not always go so smoothly. You can't control or meddle in union affairs, and union members are quite politically conscious, so the days of the completely tame company union are gone forever.

Yet I believe the entrepreneur can get the union to change its mind if he has the right attitude.

The core issue in labor-management relations is how to get your employees to speak and act as employees even when they are standing in their position as union members.

In short, the problem of labor and management basically boils down to an issue of trust. And the starting point is for the entrepreneur to win the trust of the union.

In the case of Yamato Transport, labor-management relations went steadily downhill after the twenty-four-hour strike of 1961. At the time of the Oil Shock in 1973, Yamato had about 6,500 employees, and I felt sure we were going to have to lay some of them off in order to keep the company from going under. But I really didn't want to fire anybody. So I went to the union, and this is what I said:

"Right now the good ship Yamato is caught in a terrible storm, a crisis so serious that it may very well sink. To keep it from sinking, we've got to lighten the load. I am not going to tell any of the regular crew to jump overboard. Let's get rid of everything else, except a bit of food, and tough it out. I am not going to lay any of you off, so please cooperate with me to the extent of accepting some pay cuts. I promise you that as soon as we weather this storm, I'll make it up to you."

So I completely froze all new hiring, let go of our temps and part-time workers, and we rode out the crisis. During that time I did not lay off a single regular employee. And for this the union was grateful.

Later, since we started Takkyūbin, we have been hiring large numbers of new employees every year, but as a result of this earlier experience I have made it a policy not to hire indiscriminately. Specifically, I have taken the following precautions.

First, we divide employees into three categories: regular employees, provisional employees, and contract employees. At the time of hiring, each employee is placed in one of these three categories according to the type of work we will have them do. Work that involves direct customer contact, like that of the sales drivers, is done by regular employees. Bookkeeping, sorting of parcels, and other behind-the-lines support services are as much as possible given to the provisional and contract employees. And we are working to raise the number of women employed in all of these categories. These are the basic principles.

Employees have both rights and responsibilities. The three categories were created with both the interests of the workers and the interest of the company in mind.

Regular employees work a seven-hour day, five days a week. Retirement is at age sixty. Provisional employees have the same working hours as regular employees, but their term of employment is one year, with option to renew. For the most part this is intended for working wives, who want to work for a certain period of time but don't want to make a lifelong commitment to the company. Those who do want to make a lifelong commitment can apply for regular employee status. Contract employees are people who want different working conditions from regular employees, mainly part-time employment such as a four-hour day, a three-day week, and so forth.

Why make a special point of hiring more women? In part because individually they tend to have briefer working lives as a result of marriage and child-rearing, and in part because we want to hire the best people we can find at a time when labor is in short supply. This is why I have been trying to hire more women, not only for clerical work but for all of the jobs Yamato employees do.

Another reason for the diverse categories of employees is to make it easier to shrink the work force if that should become necessary. It's a kind of safety net for the company, if you will.

As of the end of March 1999, Yamato Transport employed a total of 74,880 people. The breakdown was regular employees, 53 percent; provisional employees, 3 percent; and part-timers, including contract employees, 42 percent. As far as female workers are concerned, when we first started Takkyūbin back in 1976, they made up only 5 percent of our work force, but by March 1999 this figure had risen to 28 percent.

Firings are the biggest and most unpleasant issue for the labor union, because they affect the organization itself. Because of this, it is essential to always be thinking of ways to avoid a situation in which you have to resort to layoffs.

The union perfectly understands the fact that we are providing a safety net with the division of employees into categories. An increase in the number of employees means an increase in the number of union members. But the union does not want to deal with a sudden influx of new people; it wants to gradually expand its organization while protecting the welfare of its existing membership.

Building Trust Between Labor and Management

It was 1979 when we introduced the three categories of regular, provisional, and contract employees; but even before that, in 1972, Yamato had implemented a radical revision of its personnel system.

Up to that point, the personnel system had fundamentally divided employees into two groups based on the type of work they did: administrative (white-collar) positions on the one hand, and manual labor (blue-collar) positions on the other. The administrative track provided a path for advancement straight from the newest hires to the top positions in the company; it was set up so that with seniority and hard work you could be promoted to positions of increasing responsibility. On the other hand, the labor track—drivers, loaders, and the like—was set up so that the highest level you could be promoted to was equivalent to that of our general administrative workers—the path to executive positions was closed. The only way to become an executive was to switch over to the administrative track.

There were many individuals in the labor track, such as veteran drivers, who had a depth of experience and ability that would have allowed them to occupy positions such as depot managers—but to transfer from the labor to the administrative track you had to take a written test, and many, uncomfortable with that idea, decided to remain drivers.

As a matter of fact, the union leadership was completely dominated by blue-collar workers, and administrative workers disliked holding positions of responsibility in the union. For a blue-collar worker, becoming a union leader was a form of social advancement, and taking an equal seat at the negotiating table with the top executives of the company was a boost to their pride. Because of this, once they'd made it into the union leadership, they wanted to stay there, and to get re-elected many of them talked and acted like hard-liners in order to appeal to the union rank and file. In fact, the kind of people who became union leaders were often of outstanding ability—and often more solid thinkers than a lot of people in management.

So in 1972 we revised our personnel system, implementing a merger of the administrative and labor tracks, dropping the term manual labor altogether, and calling everyone who worked for the company "employees," regardless of the type of work they did. These changes were warmly welcomed by the union membership as a whole, and their trust in the company gradually began to increase.

There was one more point I paid attention to in cultivating the trust of the union, and that was to talk with the union leaders at every opportunity, at least in cases where it would not interfere with important management decisions.

When I was younger, I thought it was bad to consult with the union on issues of management. It was the job of the entrepreneur to work for the smooth running of the company's operations, and the job of the labor union was to press for improvements in wages and working conditions. At times, these interests were diametrically opposed, and that was why I thought the way I did.

Later, however, I began to think differently. The same individual would say different things as an employee and as a union member. But I began to wonder if this might be in part because I was discriminating between these conflicting positions as I listened to him.

Particularly from the time I began thinking of launching Takkyūbin, I made a conscious effort to consult with union leaders on planning and procedures. If you discuss things openly and frankly from the very beginning, no one is going to come away with bad feelings. But if you take the attitude that you can talk to the unions after the real decisions have already been made, you are almost certain to run into opposition and quid pro quos. I found that when I began to discuss everything in advance with the union, there began to be far fewer times when I made people feel the conflict between their position as union members and their position as employees.

For the Japanese salaryman, few things hold greater interest than rumors regarding the personnel reassignments that occur every spring in large corporations. Who is being sent where, who is being promoted to what—the rumors blossom like flowers. And it appears that union leaders, because of their frequent contact with top company executives, are often besieged with questions by employees who think they must have inside information regarding personnel matters.

At Yamato Transport, the spring often sees a personnel reshuffle at the vice-presidential level. Such important personnel changes must be voted on by the board of directors, but of course this is not the only item on the agenda at a board meeting. It often used to happen that by the time we'd finished with all the other business and left the conference room, news of the personnel changes would have already spread throughout the company. In other words, somebody on the board of directors was leaking the personnel information before the meetings had even ended. This put the union leaders in the position of hearing about these important personnel issues only after they'd made their way around the shop floor.

So here's what I did. On the day of a board meeting dealing with key personnel issues, I had the union leaders wait in a meeting room next to the boardroom. When the personnel decisions had been voted upon, I pretended to go to the bathroom, and instead went to the room where the union leaders were waiting, and let them know from the horse's mouth what the personnel decisions had been. In this way, the union leaders were the first people in the company (aside from the board itself) to know about these important personnel matters. A small point perhaps, but attention to such small points serves as a basis for building trust.

Some people believe there should be a direct pipeline between the head of the company and his counterpart in the union. But I am skeptical of this way of thinking. There is merit in the top leaders on both sides getting together to speak with total frankness and reveal their closely-held secrets to each other. But the more secret the content of their conversations becomes, the more it runs the risk of being information privately held by the two leaders, unlikely to be shared with the management team as a whole. Moreover, the top leaders may engage in subtle negotiations with one another, and this can lead to a web of mutual debts and obligations that can bind decision-makers hand and foot.

Another issue is that such meetings are likely to take place at eating and drinking establishments away from the workplace—places where it can be difficult to keep any kind of a secret. Before long it will probably become common knowledge that the leaders are meeting each other. When this happens, there will invariably be union members who see this as collusion between labor and management. As criticism of this kind grows, the apparent merits of this arrangement begin to be outweighed by its demerits.

I think it's necessary for labor and management leaders to get together to talk about things over a few drinks. But this has to be open and aboveboard. Talks without any apparent legitimate purpose, accompanied by wining and dining, really do invite charges of collusion by the rank and file.

At Yamato Transport we have a custom of throwing buffet-style parties after meetings of the health insurance association and the steering committee of the pension fund, both of which are comprised of representatives from labor and management in equal number. And it has also become customary for representatives of labor and management to go to the Yakuōin Temple at Takao in the mountains on the outskirts of Tokyo at New Year's to light a sacred fire praying for traffic safety in the coming year, and gather together around a pot of sukiyaki. Our Kanagawa branch office in Atsugi has an Inari shrine on the premises, and it has become an annual event for the president to act as the officiant for the first prayers of the year offered for the prosperity of the company, with members of labor and management sitting down together at the banquet table afterwards.

I am all for such events, when the purpose is public and straightforward—but utmost care should be taken with any kind of private meetings, to ensure that they are not misinterpreted. Paying attention to this point, and observing appropriate boundaries, will not only prevent accusations of collusion, but will also provide opportunities for a genuine exchange of views and further progress down the road to reconciliation between labor and management.

How to Take the Pulse of the Shop Floor

There are two types of information flowing through a corporation: that which flows from the top down, and that which flows from the bottom up. The flow from top downward is mainly official information, and it flows through legitimate company channels. In fact, it would not be much of an exaggeration to say that the chief function of most managerial positions is to dispense information.

On the other hand, very little of the information flowing upward passes through management positions. One of the major types of information from below is customer complaints. This is extremely important information, and needs to be transmitted immediately to the upper echelons of the company, but very little of it comes through management channels. This is because complaints reflect badly on managers, who want to conceal them, if possible.

Yet there is no information more important to the company than customer complaints. If complaints are not transmitted immediately and accurately to the top, quality control of the company's products and services goes out the window, and you get beaten by the competition. But this crucial information is something that managers do their best to sweep under the rug.

So who is it that transmits such essential information to the top executives of the company? The labor union, that's who.

In 1991 I stepped down as chairman of the board and became a consulting director of the company: not just a consultant or councillor, but a consulting director, retaining my membership on the board of directors. This was because I was worried that with the success of Takkyūbin the whole company might lose its edge and slip into complacency. If something happened and our performance started to slip, I wanted to be able to speak my piece as a member of the board.

I hadn't been in my new position for very long before I began to hear about a number of problems in the field. The bulk of them were about deliberate concealment of traffic accidents.

If there was an accident, the person involved was supposed to report it immediately to his supervisors so they could take whatever action was necessary. Depending on the circumstances, the person involved might have to pay a bit of a penalty or have it subtracted from his bonus, but there were no sanctions whatsoever against his superiors. Despite this, there were many accidents that were concealed and not reported to the company. I really couldn't comprehend the psychology behind this; maybe it's a form of behavior latent in all middle managers.

In the event of an accident, money would naturally have to be disbursed to pay for repairs to both vehicles and compensation to the other party. This money naturally came out of company funds—but this presented a real problem if you were trying to cover up the accident. So what happened was the supervisor would divert whatever funds were at his disposal—in most cases, by creating fictitious wage disbursements to part-time workers.

On the shop floor this was common knowledge. But to tell the company about this would mean informing on fellow employees, and nobody wanted to do that. So for the most part, warning of activity of this sort came to us through the labor union.

What surprised me after I became consulting director was how pervasive this problem seemed to be. It was like termites devouring the foundation of a house. I conjured up images of the company rotting from within and falling apart, and I was mortified.

So two years later, at the next board election, I swallowed my pride and returned to the position of chairman. I was determined to use my two-year term to clean up the company and re-establish the foundations of its management.

I would serve as chairman for only two years. I had absolutely no desire to hang on any longer than that as a company officer—because I felt that if I did, it would be bad for the company.

My father Yasuomi, born in 1889, lost the use of the right side of his body to paralysis in 1969, but refused to step down as president of the company. When he finally handed over the reins to me in 1971, I was forty-seven and he was already eighty-two years old. So I knew firsthand what it was like to have an elderly and increasingly incapacitated person occupying the top position. Because of this, while I still had my health, I wanted to establish a retirement age for company officers and put it into effect. In the end, I settled on sixty-three as the mandatory retirement age for the president of Yamato.

At age sixty-three I stepped down from the presidency, spent four years as chairman, and then two more after my period as consulting director. If I were to hang on any longer than this, the employees were going to get so they listened to no one but me, and this would be detrimental to the company. So in 1995 I cut all official connections with Yamato Transport.

Sometime in 1996, I happened to drop by the company headquarters on an errand, and was stopped by a labor union leader I had known before. He began, "You know, I'm hearing from the sales drivers in the field that the customers are telling them it would be a great help if Takkyūbin were open for business on New Year's Eve, New Year's Day, and January 2." He went on to say that he'd heard reports of this kind not just from one or two drivers, but from quite a large number of them.

Beginning in October 1982, Yamato had gone on a seven-day-a-week schedule, and was closed only three days out of the year: December 31 through January 2. Now this labor leader was saying that he was being asked by many of our sales drivers if we could stay open these three days as well, and have a total, 365-days-a-year operation. What he wanted to ask me was whether I thought he should bring this up at the next meeting of the joint business promotion council (Yamato's labor-management council).

I was both surprised and moved to hear this—it was evidence that communication from the shop floor was in perfect working order. And in the end, after the issue was taken up by the council, the decision was made in December 1996 to stay open 365 days a year, with no holidays.

If the proposal to do this had come from the company, I do not think the labor union would have been quick to agree. And if they did agree, it is not difficult to imagine that a number of strings might have been attached. But because it had come from the sales drivers through union channels, it was decided smoothly and without protest.

But there's another angle to this story.

Beginning in 1994, a "credit-card war" erupted between Yamato Transport and the Ministry of Posts and Telecommunications. When renewal time came round, the credit card companies were sending out the new cards as registered mail at ¥430 per unit. When Yamato introduced a similar service at ¥350, the Ministry of Posts issued us a warning, saying delivery of credit cards by Takkyūbin was in violation of the Postal Law. This was the beginning.

Yamato, for its part, contended that credit cards were not correspondence, while the ministry insisted that they were, and delivery of them by any other organization than the Japanese postal service was a violation of the Postal Law, carrying a maximum penalty of three years imprisonment. When Yamato demonstrated its willingness to be indicted and then fight the case in court, the ministry began marketing a new ¥240 "delivery confirmation service." Yamato was not interested in cutting its rates any further to continue the battle, so the credit-card war thus came to a natural conclusion.

The labor union, which had long called for privatization of the postal service, indicated at this point that it was ready to throw the weight of its entire organization behind a fight with the ministry. And in order to be prepared to possibly take over delivery of the New Year's mail, keeping Yamato open through the New Year's holidays had been written into its official program for action. This would later prove valuable in smoothing the transition to 365-days-per-year operations.

Two Hearts Beating as One

Yamato Transport's labor union was founded in 1946. My father believed that, with the war over, democracy was going to be the order of the day and that the creation of labor unions was inevitable. So rather than have it set up by outside agitators, he encouraged the development of a healthy union within the company.

Because it was a company union, it was basically a pretty tame one. But because it was connected with a larger transport industry union affiliated with Sōhyō (the General Council of Trade Unions of Japan), it had to engage in the yearly round of work slowdowns and so forth in order to show its solidarity. The employees all had a strong sense of belonging to the company, but as union members they had to talk the union talk, which set my teeth on edge.

From the time we started Takkyūbin in 1976, in part because we were suddenly in a different sort of business than the other companies and unions in the industry, the Yamato union began to adopt a more cooperative attitude.

This tendency was strengthened by the fact that changes had also occurred in the way the company thought about the union. Before, when the union was seen as an organization set up in opposition to the company, policy veered between confrontation and compromise. Improvement of the working conditions of employees was an important theme for management in a labor-intensive industry such as transport, but it was felt that this should be pursued very cautiously, and the tempo of change dropped further and further behind the demands of the union. This was one of the reasons the union came to distrust the company, feeling that there was always a lot of slick maneuvering in the company's approach.

But with the launch of Takkyūbin, I decided to make the foundation of my policy toward the union one of trying to convince it that the company and the union shared a common fate. So I made a concerted effort to avoid anything that might appear to be maneuvering in the eyes of the union.

In return for management sharing with labor a commitment to the policy and objectives of improving working conditions, both labor and management would have to share responsibility for the methods used to achieve this end. As this way of thinking began to permeate the company, the sense of solidarity between labor and management was strengthened. One development that symbolized this new-found unity was the response of Yamato Transport's union to the opposition to deregulation announced in February 1985 by its umbrella organization, the All-Japan Federation of Transport Worker's Unions. Yamato's union requested that this policy item be removed from the federation's action program. From this point forward, Yamato's union began to express its own unique opinions with greater confidence, and to try to square the program of labor with the policies of the company.

Then, in the 1996 general elections, the union mobilized its entire organization in support of Prime Minister Hosokawa Morihiro and his agreement to privatize the postal service, as well as candidates such as Koizumi Jun'ichirō of the Liberal Democratic Party.

The company and the union are two hearts beating as one, like husband and wife. When they are united behind the direction and strategies of management, this can provide a powerful motive force for challenging the intense competition of today's market economy. To achieve such unity of purpose is difficult, but not impossible. It may not happen overnight, but with continued effort and attention to the details, it can definitely be accomplished.

Business Differentiation

B usiness differentiation involves the establishment of a unique form of enterprise, or business type. For example, in the business category of "retail," supermarkets and convenience stores represent two distinct business types.

Takkyūbin was a completely new business type, radically different from existing freight trucking operations. Because of this, we had to invent and develop new hardware, software, and humanware. In order to adapt to the new type of service Takkyūbin was providing, we enlisted the help of experts in various fields and conceived, implemented, and improved upon everything from the design of our delivery vans and parcel-sorting equipment to our information system for dispatching and tracking, and even our operations manual for the sales drivers.

The process of business differentiation tests the wisdom and ingenuity of the entrepreneur. In this chapter we will look at how clearly grasping the uniqueness of your enterprise and making a wholehearted commitment to business differentiation can be the key to success or failure.

What is Business Differentiation?

In recent years business differentiation has become a bit of a buzzword. In the past, you could tell people what general line of business you were in, but now, as different business types have proliferated within the same industry, it has become ever more necessary to differentiate your business type from others in the same field.

Let's look at some typical examples of different business types. Use of the term "business differentiation" originated in the retail industry, I believe, and the first business types to attract attention were large-scale retail operations, particularly supermarkets.

Supermarkets made a spectacular appearance on the scene at the height of the distribution revolution. As the standard-bearer for the mass marketing that was needed to link mass production with mass consumption, the supermarket chains expanded rapidly, with the goal of achieving sufficient market share to be able to determine retail prices. In every part of the country they competed with established local retailers, and won a truly revolutionary victory.

Volume buying and volume sales made it possible to lower prices drastically. A total commitment to volume retail as a business type was what made the supermarkets prosper.

However, with the passage of nearly half a century, so many supermarkets had sprung up that the result was excessive competition, declining profits, and in some cases, store closures.

At the same time, a new business type pushed its way to the fore: the convenience store. The convenience stores, many of which began as subsidiaries of major supermarkets, rapidly grew into chains with thousands of outlets, and have become major corporations rivaling and even surpassing the supermarket giants of the past as the stars of the retail industry.

What lay behind this was the development of a unique business type, based on the following characteristics: A massive number of outlets in order to dominate extremely narrow market spheres. A broad and continually changing inventory. Open 24 hours a day, 365 days a year. A system of frequent restocking—commonly several times a day. Transactions handled at the register by a small sales staff. What all this represented was a thoroughgoing effort to make "convenience" a reality—an effort that resulted in overwhelming success in the intensely competitive retail industry.

Another example is the rapid growth of a business type known in Japan as "roadside shops" (similar to outlet stores in the United States) in the outlying areas of Japan's major cities. These enterprises have become a pillar of the distribution revolution by building large outlets in suburban areas where land prices are comparatively cheap, and featuring huge inventories at major discount. The "roadside shops" began with menswear and auto parts, but have expanded into sales of books, eyeglasses, shoes, and other products, and this new business type has attracted much consumer attention.

Of course business differentiation is not something that began yesterday. It has long been a fact of life in the restaurant industry, for instance. The Sapporo *ramen* chain right after the war, Yoshinoya and its *gyūdon*, and more recently the self-service coffee franchises such as Doutor and Starbucks are all examples of companies that have succeeded in business differentiation and the establishment of a unique identity.

There are various examples of differentiation in the transport business as well: specialists in transport of petrochemicals with tanker trucks, and vendors of cement with their fleets of cement mixers come to mind. The latter is a truly unique idea: a system in which the product is actually being manufactured during transport!

What all these examples tell us is that business differentiation means focusing on a market and aiming at total efficiency in serving that market, with the goal of establishing a decisive advantage over your competitors in terms of service and cost.

When it came to Takkyūbin I was dismayed to find that many people— even in the trucking industry—saw it as the same business type as ordinary mixed-lot freight trucking. From the time I launched Takkyūbin in 1976, my goal was to develop a new business type, fundamentally different from commercial mixed-lot freight.

Existing small parcel mixed-lot shipping—also known as LTL (less-than-load) shipping—involves contracts with clients to transport freight along predetermined routes. It's essentially the same as a passenger bus service. On the other hand, you have regional freight transport, also known as charter-by-truckload or simply TL carriers, who provide exclusive chartered service for specific clients—the equivalent of a taxi or a hired car.

Until the advent of Takkyūbin, both de jure and de facto there were only these two types of trucking (LTL and TL). Takkyūbin represented a third, entirely different business type.

Takkyūbin would take parcels from the general public, feed them into a pre-established transport system, and deliver them anywhere in the country. This was a service identical to that of the Japanese postal service's small parcel service—one that had not existed in the field of truck transport up to that point. Takkyūbin's business type was an effort to create a new system fusing hardware, software, and humanware—a total system, integrating the component systems of collection, transport, and delivery.

Takkyūbin began with the collection of parcels from the general public by our sales drivers (SD). This was a process that had not existed in trucking prior to that time. But you couldn't get anywhere without first collecting the freight.

The pillars of the collection system were the development of special "walkthrough" vans for collection and delivery, the creation of an operations manual for the SDs, and the training of these sales drivers. Concurrently we worked to develop a network of agents and a system for managing it.

The freight collected by the trucks or by the agents was consolidated at our centers, where the destination center for each parcel was determined and an appropriate code number attached. Parcels readied in this way were loaded onto transfer trucks bound for the bases, where they would be prepared for shipment according to region. All of this process I have just related constituted the collection system.

The transport system began at the bases, where automated equipment sorted the parcels according to destination, after which they were loaded onto long-haul trucks. Naturally the establishment of a schedule for these freight runs and a system for managing them was an essential part of this. As soon as the long-haul trucks arrived at their destination base, their cargoes would be transferred to the delivery centers.

The delivery system began with the sorting and loading of these parcels into the appropriate delivery vans. After that, the SDs would carry out the final process of delivery, and the system was complete.

We also created a consistent information system linking these three systems of collection, transport, and delivery that was able to check the flow through the entire system to make sure that no parcels went off-course.

Working with Toyota to Develop the Walkthrough Van

From a user's point of view freight trucks had always left a lot to be desired. I had never been satisfied with them.

Any truck manufacturer will tell you, "Our trucks have powerful engines, they're built tough enough to stand a bit of overloading, and they get good gas mileage—they're good trucks." There are certainly people who would agree that these factors make a good truck. But I don't.

To me a good truck is fundamentally one that is easy to load and unload, easy for the driver to get in and out of, and which has a cargo bed that is easy to work on. If you look at it from this point of view, I don't think there is a truck on the market that really measures up.

The whole purpose of a truck is to load cargo and transport it. Of course you want it to run economically. But loading cargo is an absolute requirement. It may run fine—but if it's not carrying any cargo, it is not earning any money. Ease of use in the work process is more important than how well it runs. Particularly in a labor-intensive industry like transport, the biggest priority has to be on ease of use, which equates to greater work efficiency and thus savings in terms of labor.

The large trucks currently on the market, even though they are built for the purpose of carrying large-volume cargos, have had so little thought put into the problem of how to load and unload them that they seem to be saying, "Figure it out for yourself." In recent years a number of trucks have come out that have incorporated tailgate lifts, but development of truck bodies suitable for containerization and of doubles trailers has lagged in many respects.

Small delivery vans are made in such a way that workers keep bumping their heads inside the cargo compartment. This also irritated me. Don't the manufacturers care that the only way you can work inside their trucks is hunched over in an unnatural position?

In addition, it is dangerous for the driver of a truck to have to get out of it on the right side, facing traffic. In Japan we drive on the left, so the driver should get out on the left. The front passenger seat prevents this. But is it necessary? The vast majority of vans you see driving around town are carrying only a driver—especially professional transport company vans. Since the manufacturers are making trucks with the same mindset as making cars, they have put an unnecessary seat in the trucks. Take away the passenger seat, and you make it possible to exit the truck on the left—for a tremendous gain not only in safety but in work efficiency.

Takkyūbin work requires the SDs to be constantly getting in and out of their trucks—eighty times a day is nothing unusual. If you are getting out on the right, first you have to make sure nobody's behind you, open the door, get out, and walk around to the left-hand sidewalk. With no passenger seat you can get directly out of the left side onto the sidewalk. This saves a lot of time. If you save fifteen seconds every time you get in and out of the truck, and you do that eighty times a day, you save twenty minutes. If you compute this over a year's time, the savings in personnel costs is no laughing matter.

Takkyūbin's walkthrough vans (manufactured by Toyota Motors under the brand name Quick Delivery) are called that because the driver can enter the cargo bay directly from the driver's area. In regular vans, the driver usually has to get out, walk around to the rear of the vehicle, and open the rear doors to access the cargo compartment. This takes time and effort, and if it is raining, both the driver and the cargo are likely to get wet. With

Takkyūbin's vans, the SD can enter the cargo bay directly from the driver's area, locate the parcel he needs, exit through the left-hand door, and make his delivery. The cargo bay has also been equipped with a refrigerator for Cool Takkyūbin. And since the driver's area also serves as the SD's office, it is equipped with a radio, a cashbox, a writing ledge, and so on. The cargo bay has a high roof—no SD has ever hit his head on one.

When we wanted to develop a van exclusively for Takkyūbin we discussed it with manufacturers we were already doing business with, but didn't get favorable responses from any of them. We were in a fix, but Toyota Motors, which we had never dealt with before, was willing to talk with us, and then willing to take on the development project. Yamato employees made a model out of plywood and explained thoroughly what we were after. Toyota then made preliminary sketches and produced a prototype, which, with various revisions, was turned into the finished product.

Since Toyota had gone through such trouble for us in producing this special-order vehicle, we went with them as our sole supplier of the walk-through trucks. When other manufacturers saw the new vans, they all came to us insisting that they could make something similar—but they had missed their chance.

As of the end of March 1999, Yamato owned a fleet of some 24,000 delivery vans, and almost all of them were made by Toyota. Until the walk-through truck, Toyota had never done business with us—but they sure seized a good business opportunity when they saw it.

The Introduction of Automated Sorting

When we were launching Takkyūbin, we faced the issue of whether or not to introduce automatic sorting equipment. At the time, no such machines were in practical use in Japan. In the factories, of course, various automated assembly lines had been created, and conveyor systems of one kind or another were certainly not unusual. But in the trucking industry, automation had not amounted to much more than occasional use of a conveyor system known as a towveyor. The towveyor operated something like a cable car: an endless chain loop set into a track in the floor towed carts filled with parcels from one part of the loading area to another. We don't use them much anymore.

With Takkyūbin, we had to sort an enormous volume of parcels by destination within an extremely limited time frame. For this purpose, automated sorting seemed not only useful, but essential. Some research revealed that there were two basic types of automated freight-sorting machines: ones based on diverters and ones based on trays.

Diverter systems involved running the parcels on a conveyor belt, from which mechanical arms called diverters would, at intervals, send parcels down chutes designated for specific destinations. All this was controlled from the head of the conveyor belt by an operative called a keyer, who would read the destination code number on each package as it came down the line, and use a keyboard to activate the appropriate diverter to shove it down the designated chute.

In the tray systems, parcels were placed in shallow trays about fifty centimeters (twenty inches) in diameter, traveling on an endless conveyor belt, and the destination chute number was keyed in at that point. When it reached the designated chute, the tray would make a 90° turn and drop into the chute with its parcels.

Both methods had their strengths and weaknesses, and it was difficult to choose between them, but since Takkyūbin was going to be handling parcels that were not of a standardized size, we settled on the diverter system, which we imported from the Swedish firm Sandvig.

Both types of equipment were supposed to be able to sort seven to eight thousand parcels an hour, but because there was a limit to the speed at which the keyer could read the destination codes and key the chute numbers, in reality such numbers were not possible. A single keyer could actually handle about three thousand parcels an hour; a pair could handle six thousand.

At present, each of Yamato Transport's bases is equipped with two Sandvig automatic sorting lines. And interestingly enough, every base also operates two manual sorting lines. The manual lines are a simple belt conveyor with a line of operators standing on both sides, with each man pulling off parcels headed for the destinations for which he is responsible.

The manual lines can handle the same volume of packages in an hour as the automated lines. The reason we have the manual lines is because fragile parcels can be damaged in the automated lines. Another reason is that the manual lines have demonstrated greater dependability and efficiency than their automated counterparts when sorting at peak volume periods.

Our initial plans assumed that if we introduced automatic sorting equipment, it would be able to handle rush periods when a large volume of material had to be sorted in a short time. But when we actually got it up and running, we found that during peak periods such as the morning rush when the long-haul trucks were all arriving, the manual lines were able to sort a far larger number of parcels. Of course they also required significantly more manpower, but what we needed above all else was speed. And here we found that throwing personnel at the problem—human wave tactics—actually worked.

So when do we run the automatic lines? During the day, late at night, and in the early morning when the long-haul trucks are only arriving sporadically. The advantage is that during these time slots, we can run a fully automated process that requires only one keyer.

In the beginning, we introduced automated sorting because we thought it would be faster and require fewer personnel. But when we actually used it, we found that the automated equipment was not necessarily faster. The manual system actually demonstrated a superior sorting capacity. Of course the automated equipment was better from the standpoint of labor-saving, but because it was also more likely to damage fragile parcels, it was clear that we could not depend on it exclusively. So in the end we concluded that using both automated and manual systems was the best idea.

Back when Yamato still did not have enough bases set up, for a while we leased the Hazawa freight terminal in Yokohama from JR Freight. The Hazawa terminal was close to Shin Yokohama station, and had been built during the war by the Japanese National Railways (JNR) as a collection, sorting, and delivery hub for small- and medium-sized parcels. They had been thorough in their use of the latest labor-saving devices, and it was famous as an automated facility, but in fact the war came to an end before it was ever used, and billions of yen worth of equipment was abandoned to rust.

JR Freight wasn't using it, so they were happy to lease it to us when we asked. When I went to inspect it, I was amazed. Parcels brought by freight trains from all over Japan were to have been offloaded from the freight cars into wheeled containers pulled on a completely automated towveyor system through an underground tunnel to an adjoining sorting platform. The containers would then be hoisted above a conveyor line, where they were turned upside down and their contents dumped onto the line. In the past I'd seen fully loaded coal carts upended into coal cars at a railway siding, but these would have been parcels! With a setup like this, packages were bound to be damaged. Then, the parcels continued down the conveyor line, where they were to be automatically sorted for destination. The station was indeed almost fully automated. JNR liked hardware solutions, and I had heard they had built unmanned freight yards, but when I actually saw this freight station I was amazed at the almost religious devotion to the omnipotence of hardware that it represented. Parcels are not coal, and dumping them from midair onto a conveyor belt—what were they thinking?

In any case, we had all the old automated equipment removed, and leased the facility as a venue for Yamato's own human-wave approach. But I felt like I had a chance to see in the starkest terms the flaws of the old JNR.

Systems are built out of a fusion of hardware, software, and human-ware, and I think the human element is particularly important. If you get the human element right, the entire system will be the better for it.

The Information System

One of the things I put special energy into as we proceeded with building Takkyūbin as a business was the construction of its information system. Why? Because parcels can neither talk nor walk.

Ask a Takkyūbin parcel where it wants to go, and you are not likely to get an answer. So if the destinations of these parcels that are going all over the country are not clearly indicated, we have a problem. Nor is that enough. Once they reach the destination, they have to be loaded individually into vans and delivered, so we need a precise local address to make sure they get onto the right van. And if we can't respond to requests from the sender for information on tracking and time of delivery, we are not really providing the best service.

The information system is what takes care of all this. You can see why the information system is extremely important, as important as our work procedures.

At Yamato, we call Takkyūbin's information system the NEKO system (from the Japanese word for cat, since our trademark is a black cat). NEKO 1.0 was launched along with Takkyūbin, and now, with successive changes and upgrades, we are running NEKO 4.0.

The NEKO system begins with the input of the waybill number on a parcel into our mainframe computer. In the beginning, this inputting was quite primitive—done at desktop terminals in our centers, using punch-cards. In 1980 we switched to NEKO 2.0, a system in which the waybill numbers were given as bar codes that could be input with a scanner, which was a immense saving in terms of labor. Another hardware innovation was the introduction of Takkyūbin terminals at all of our branches throughout the country. With this online network, we could have accurate figures the next day on how many parcels we had collected on a given day, and it really began to demonstrate its power as a tool for supporting corporate strategy.

NEKO 3.0 began beta testing in 1985 and was implemented company-wide the following year. With it, every SD was given a portable POS terminal that allowed him to input collection and delivery data on the spot. There were also workstations set up at the centers that allowed SDs returning from their rounds to immediately uplink information to our regional clusters and on to our central mainframe. As a result, we were able to diversify and operate a more integrated program of services, offering new ones such as Golf Takkyūbin and Ski Takkyūbin.

I'll discuss this further in chapter 12, but Golf and Ski Takkyūbin differed from our normal service because next-day delivery was not the goal. Once received, the parcels for these services have to be held at one of our centers, and delivered to the golf course or ski resort on the day prior to their intended use. Computerized tracking makes it possible to provide our customers with accurate and up-to-date information on these shipments.

In 1993 we upgraded to the NEKO 4.0 system we are currently running. The SDs were issued new hand-held POS terminals capable of automatically determining and printing out the code number of the delivery center they were bound for once the SD entered the destination address at the time of pickup. This printed code could then be affixed to the parcel, which not only saved effort, but also eliminated the possibility of misloading due to mistaken coding—both of which contributed to improvements in our level of service.

A receipt could also be issued to the sender at the time of pickup, and the new system also made it easy to calculate the portion of the shipping fee owed to our agents. The accuracy of our tracking system was improved, making it possible to give prompt and correct responses to customer queries.

In addition, our efforts to improve service were further enhanced by putting into operation a new collection dispatching system. With this system, all we needed was the customer's phone number and we could access their name and address and immediately dispatch one of our vans in the area to pick up their parcel. Not only did this speed dispatching, it also allowed us to estimate the time of the pickup and inform the customer of this, so that we were able to save more customers from the experience of waiting impatiently for the Black Cat van to show up.

NEKO 5.0 is presently being prepared for implementation during the 1999 fiscal year. When that happens, the SDs will be carrying miniaturized, ultralight terminals that will provide a new level of convenience for the SDs and for our customers.

By the way, while we are talking about hardware, as of March 1999 we have two mainframe computers (a main unit in Osaka and a backup in Tokyo), 49 regional cluster computers, 3,000 workstations, 33,700 handheld terminals, and 4,500 operations terminals.

The systems that have powered Takkyūbin's business differentiation—the walkthrough vans, the automatic sorting equipment, the information system—have all been developed with the assistance of specialists, but fundamentally they have been conceived, built, and modified by Yamato Transport employees. A business type is not something somebody can teach you—you have to make it your own.

Then, the parcels continued down the conveyor line, where they were to be automatically sorted for destination. The station was indeed almost fully automated. The National Railways liked hardware solutions.....

New Product Development

In this chapter I will discuss Yamato Transport's approach to new product development.

At present, the Takkyūbin product lineup covers a broad range, from Ski Takkyūbin and Golf Takkyūbin to Cool Takkyūbin (delivery of refrigerated and frozen goods), Collect Service (delivery of mail-order goods in a collect-on-delivery format), and Book Service (order and delivery of books).

These products are very different from our general Takkyūbin service. Like the development of business types I discussed in chapter 11, they required the creation of new hardware and software systems. Some of them, like Cool Takkyūbin, required an enormous commitment to new capital investment. What encouraged us to make that commitment, developing new products one after the other, following the motto "First service, then profits," was our success in accurately reading the latent demand of our customers.

Henceforth, as Internet-based marketing expands, I expect to see a whole new range of opportunities for business development centered around our core Takkyūbin operation.

Ski Takkyūbin

In fiscal 1980, five years after our launch of Takkyūbin in 1976, we finally started turning a profit—in fact, a pretax profit of a bit over 5 percent. During the entire period we had worked hard at differentiating our service under the slogan "First service, then profits."

We also steadily expanded our area of operations from our initial base in the Kantō region, and developed our information system so that we could respond immediately to customer queries concerning the status of their shipments. But as we were working in this way to improve our basic Takkyūbin service, we were also pouring energy into the development of new services.

The first of these new services was Ski Takkyūbin, which commenced operations on December 1, 1983. The idea originated with an employee in our Nagano branch, who suggested that customers would be pleased with what he called a "travel-light" ski service. It's not surprising that such an unusual concept would come from an employee in Nagano, where the snow and the ski resorts are plentiful.

After the war, when things had settled down a bit, there was a ski boom. Ski resorts were built all over the place, along with the attendant hotels and bed-and-breakfasts. JNR even added trains to their schedule to transport skiers to the slopes. Soon the trains were crammed with skiers, skis, backpacks, and whatnot—and since Tokyo's Ueno station was the point of departure for trains to the ski areas, the crowding on the Yamanote and Chūō line commuter trains serving Ueno was made even worse by the skiers and their equipment, inconveniencing the other passengers.

If skis, backpacks, and other equipment could be sent ahead by Takkyūbin, the skiers could travel light, carrying no luggage; and the other passengers could travel without worrying about getting poked by skis or ski poles. But Takkyūbin had a size limit on the packages it would accept—the sum of the length, width, and depth of the package had to be less than a meter—and skis fell outside this limit. Skis also had to be transported and stored vertically to avoid damage. All in all, they were difficult to handle, and we had avoided them up to this point.

The Nagano branch ran a five-month test of the service from December to April of 1982, and customer response was highly favorable: in five months the service was used 17,000 times. So we decided to put the full weight of the company behind the idea. In its first year Ski Takkyūbin had 205,000 users and became a new pillar of our business.

But toward the end of the following year, 1984, we ran into major trouble. The delivery base designated for our Ski Takkyūbin operations in Nagano Prefecture was our newly constructed Nagaoka base, located near the Nagaoka interchange on the Kan'etsu Freeway. We chose Nagaoka over the more direct route via National Highway 18 over Usui Pass on the border between Gunma and Nagano prefectures, because in winter the pass would sometimes be blocked by snow. However, on Christmas Eve of 1984 there was a blizzard of major proportions, completely stopping travel on the road between our Nagaoka base and the freeway interchange. None of the trucks loaded with skis could reach the base, and delivery of the skis to the Nagano ski resorts was completely cut off.

In a panic, we pulled employees off of their year-end holiday and mobilized an emergency team, but even this human-wave tactic was of no avail against the worst blizzard in many years, and we ended up disappointing twenty or thirty thousand customers.

We made emergency calls to all the hotels and other accommodations, apologizing to our customers and promising to reimburse them for the cost of rental skis and even for the socks and fresh underclothes they had to buy since their luggage had not been delivered.

As a result, we had few of the complaints we had feared, and in fact, the promptness and sincerity of our response must have won us a fair amount of goodwill, for the following year we had more Ski Takkyūbin customers than ever before.

This mishap cost us more than a billion yen, but the company policy was to spare no expense in rectifying the situation, and words cannot express my gratitude to the employees who gave so unstintingly of their time and effort in order to do so. I was also really delighted that this became an opportunity for all of our employees to take to heart the lesson that a prompt and honest response to a problem will win the kind of trust that money can't buy.

Another lesson learned was to be prepared for a recurrence, and so we gradually built a system for dealing with another heavy snowfall, including the purchase of a fleet of snowmobiles. In addition, we opened new centers at the ski resorts of Ishiuchi in the Jōetsu area of Niigata Prefecture and at Niseko in Hokkaidō. Our competitors couldn't figure out what Yamato Transport was up to, building shipping facilities up in the mountains miles from any factory, but when the snow began to fall and young people from the cities lined up toting skis and eager to pay for shipping them, I think maybe they got the picture.

For most people in the transport business, snow is nothing but a problem, but for Yamato Transport, snow means income—so let it snow, let it snow, let it snow!

Golf Takkyūbin

Golf Takkyūbin was launched at almost the same time as Ski Takkyūbin, in April 1984.

In postwar Japan, golf enjoyed an even greater boom than skiing. Like skiing, it involves equipment that is a real pain to lug around. We realized that it would be a lot more convenient for people if they could send their clubs and other equipment via Takkyūbin. The question was how to turn this idea into a product.

In the case of Golf Takkyūbin, it was clear that the demand would be there—but there were difficult obstacles to developing it as a product. First of all, you had to make sure you delivered to the right golf course. You wouldn't think this would be a problem, since it's hard to lose a golf course—but you'd be wrong.

There are an awful lot of golf courses with similar names: Fuji Golf Course, Fuji Country Club, Fuji Golf Club, and so on. And to make matters worse, the golfers themselves often don't know the correct name of the course they intend to play on. They don't realize that their course might be near one with a very similar name. So frequently the destination they fill in on the waybill turns out to be useless. "It's going to Tsurugashima," they'll say, but if you ask them whether they mean the country club or the golf course, there is a good chance they won't be able to tell you.

This is a pretty important point. Golf equipment is not for next-day delivery. Most people using the service bring their bags to a Takkyūbin office three or four days before they intend to play. If we delivered them the next day to the golf course, the managers of the course would yell at us. Clubhouses at any course are not that large, and most of them only have space for the equipment of the people actually playing that day—so delivering clubs for a customer who is not going to be playing for another two or three days is simply a hassle for them. So we can't really deliver until the day before scheduled play. Despite this fact, customers will still call several days in advance to see if the clubs have arrived at the clubhouse, and worry when they have not. So we have to inform the clubhouse that we are holding the clubs at one of our business locations and will deliver them the day prior to the scheduled round. On the other hand, if the clubs don't arrive on the scheduled day, there's big trouble. You can see how even something like delivering some golf clubs is really not as simple as it sounds.

In addition, golf clubs need to be transported and stored in an upright position to avoid damage. But they are also top-heavy and tend to fall over easily, so they are a pain to handle. Many of them are also quite valuable, and huge problems would result if they were mistakenly switched with someone else's set.

On top of everything else, there are issues with the return shipment. When the customers have finished play, the golf course hands their clubs over to the contracted shipping company. When this company is Yamato, there is no problem, but there are golf courses that are owned by conglomerates and will not hand clubs over to any shipping company that is not part of their business group. In extreme cases, they will even refuse to allow vans from other shipping companies on their premises. In such cases, even if the customer specifies that they want to use Takkyūbin, we cannot serve them. So when they come off an enjoyable day on the links, they have to go through all the trouble of stopping at the front desk to write out their address, pay for shipping, and so on.

So we decided to contact the other companies handling golf bag deliveries and work out round-trip service arrangements. Now, when you had Takkyūbin transport your golf clubs from your home to the course, you would also order the return shipping, fill out the waybill, pay the fee and get a ¥100 discount for doing so. If you happen to be playing at a course where Takkyūbin is not contracted for pickup, the contracted company will pick up the clubs and take them to their nearest depot where Yamato will pick them up and handle the delivery to your home.

This cooperation between companies, giving priority to the needs of the consumer over their own individual profit or loss, is laudable. And if this plants in the consumer's mind the habit of using parcel services—regardless of the company—to transport their golf clubs, then it is also good for the transport industry as a whole.

Whether it is ski equipment or golf clubs, dependable transport via Takkyūbin requires the creation of a reliable information system. In fact, today's Ski Takkyūbin and Golf Takkyūbin are the result of an integrated effort at business differentiation, combining development of the hardware necessary to transport and store these items in a vertical position, creation of an information system and backup systems to support the deliveries, and a siting strategy for building delivery centers in the mountain and resort areas where the ski slopes, hotels, and golf courses are located. Though these services are grounded in the Takkyūbin concept, I think you can see how we have built them into distinct business types in their own right.

Cool Takkyūbin

Cool Takkyūbin is certainly a type of Takkyūbin service, but it, too, is something we have developed as a distinct business type.

One hot summer day I walked along the loading dock at one of our bases, lost in thought.

Once upon at time, offices at transport companies used to be really hot. The business depended on paperwork—waybills, invoices, etc.—and fans might scatter them all over the place. So fans were banned, and boy, was it hot. But what about now? Now, all our offices are air conditioned. No matter how hot it gets outside we can work in comfort. It's like another world.

When we get home from work, we also have air conditioning. No matter where we are, at home or on the job, we now keep cool in air-conditioned comfort. But what about freight? At the height of the summer, almost anywhere in Japan the daytime temperature will hit 35° C (95° F). Inside a truck sitting in the blazing sun, the temperature can rise above 50° C (122° F). The poor parcels are suffering all day long in such heat. Isn't there any way we can make them feel cool?

Especially since many of the parcels handled by Takkyūbin contain fresh food and produce, keeping them cool is actually necessary in terms of quality control. I was sure if we started offering refrigerated service, it would give us a tremendous sales advantage, and bring in more revenue.

I first put together a Cool Takkyūbin project team to research the idea in 1985, about the time of our second Frontrunner's Three-Year Plan. At the time, huge amounts of chilled beef were being imported from Australia via refrigerated container ships. NYK and other container manufacturers had formed a team to study refrigerated containers. We obtained various data from them, and thought about the Cool Takkyūbin concept.

Meat and fish keep best when chilled—that is, in an environment of 0°–2° C (32°–36° F). For vegetables, the optimum temperature range is 5°–10° C (41°–50° F). Ice cream and other frozen foods need to be at temperatures below −18° C (0° F). At the time, the refrigerators on the consumer market all had three-temperature range capability.

With Takkyūbin, we also decided to go, ideally, with three ranges: cold, chilled, and frozen. To make this possible, the collection and delivery vans, the centers, and the long-haul trucks would all have to be equipped with three-range refrigeration units. When we contacted the manufacturers, they said they could make them any size we wanted. The problem was the electric power source.

The vans were small, and especially on summer days, if their engines were also taxed by running electric power to the refrigerator, they would overheat. And the trailers for the long-haul trucks connecting our bases were leased from other companies, so naturally they did not have power supplies for refrigeration.

There was of course no problem putting refrigerators in our centers and bases, but unless we could equip the trucks with them, we could not provide door-to-door refrigerated transport.

There was nothing to be done. We gave up on the idea of electric refrigeration. What could we substitute for it? With a bit of research we learned that some amazingly effective refrigerants had been developed, and after a number of tests, we settled on this as the way to implement Cool Takkyūbin.

When you think of refrigerants, dry ice comes to mind, but it is unsuitable for use in refrigerated transport. Why? Because it is too cold. It's fine for ice cream and other frozen foods, but with meat and fish, any portion exposed to dry ice will freeze and be spoiled. Moreover, since it is difficult to ensure proper circulation within the storage unit of the dry ice that has evaporated and formed gas, an equal temperature distribution cannot be maintained. So dry ice is not very good from the standpoint of temperature control. Yamato Transport uses dry ice only as a backup. The aim of Cool Takkyūbin was not to provide an exclusive refrigerated or frozen transport service, but to provide for temperature-controlled shipments as a part of a regular transport and delivery service.

When we began development, I gave the project team the following five guidelines:

1. The object is goods being sent from producers or stores to individual consumers.
2. We will handle any type of packaging.
3. There should be a choice of several temperature ranges appropriate to the articles being shipped.
4. We should not cause the clients any additional labor or expense.
5. The service should be available anywhere and everywhere.

Based on the project team's research, we began test marketing in August 1987. In the beginning, we restricted delivery to the twenty-three wards of Tokyo, and senders to the eight areas of Sendai, Nagaoka, Chiba, Yokohama, Atsugi, Shizuoka, Osaka-Kobe, and Okayama. Response was enthusiastic, and we found no problems with our quality control.

So beginning in July 1988, we expanded service nationwide, with the exception of the island of Shikoku. From April 1988 through March 1989 we handled more than 8.6 million refrigerated shipments, which increased to 19 million the following year. We were off to a good start.

Launching Cool Takkyūbin required an enormous capital investment. Our rough estimate was that it would take more than ¥30 billion, but our motto was "First service, then profits." I gave the go-ahead without asking for more precise numbers. I knew the demand would be there, and I had confidence that we could corner the market in shipping fresh food and produce.

Since launching Cool Takkyūbin, our fixed capital investment (excluding expendables such as refrigerants) in refrigerators, freezer cabinets, deep freezes, refrigerated sorting rooms, coolers, cold boxes, and the like has amounted to roughly ¥45 billion.

On the other hand, Cool Takkyūbin now handles about 970 billion units a year, with revenues of more than a trillion yen annually, accounting for 12.5 percent of all Takkyūbin shipments and 18 percent of total revenue.

Cool Takkyūbin has had a major change since its inception. We began with three temperature ranges, but now offer only two: refrigerated (3°C; 37.4° F) and frozen (-18°C; 0° F). The launch of Cool Takkyūbin came right after three-range refrigerators hit the market, and we were influenced by the heavy advertising appliance makers were putting into their capacity for chilled food. This may be desirable for refrigerators used in the home, but we found that for transport, two temperature ranges were sufficient. In other words, we decided to "chill out" on "chilled."

Collect Service

The volume of freight Takkyūbin handles has grown steadily—and dramatically. One reason for this has been the growth in mail-order business.

Mail-order shopping has been a big hit in Japan, spurred by the increasing number of working housewives and the convenience of home delivery versus the time and effort involved in going to the store. It is now available for almost every type of product imaginable.

Mail-order businesses solicit for orders via catalogue distribution or the mass media, and may or may not hold extensive inventories, but in any case ship the goods as soon as they receive orders. For this they were using Takkyūbin, but payment was received after the fact, via bank transfers, postal money orders, and the like. This involved a significant degree of risk, and was a problem for the mail-order companies.

At Yamato Transport, we noticed this, and saw a business opportunity in the collection of these payments. Shipping companies had long been collecting payment for goods they delivered, calling it collect-on-delivery, or C.O.D. Yamato Transport had been delivering for the major department stores in Tokyo since before the war, and had long-standing business relations with them that included regular C.O.D. service.

A customer might see something they wanted at the department store, but not have the cash to buy it. In such cases they would use the C.O.D. service. Now that credit cards have become so common, hardly anyone uses this type of service anymore, but back in the day it was a major part of the work of Yamato's department store division. The system was pretty primitive back then: payment for the items was seen as the department store's money and never entered Yamato's accounting—it was kept in a separate envelope and returned to the store in a reverse of the process of delivery.

Nowadays the clients are mail-order companies, and we figured that if we collected payment for them at the time we delivered the goods, it would reduce trouble and risk for both the mail-order businesses and their customers, and make them both happy.

If that was the case, maybe we could go one step further, and actually purchase the accounts receivable from the mail-order company when they handed the goods over to us for delivery—in other words, engage in factoring.

But that would get us into one end of the finance business, and the Finance Ministry would probably give us grief. So we gave up on that idea and decided the best approach was to promise to transfer payment to the mail-order business within a week of receiving the goods from them for delivery.

This was the concept that was refined into our Collect Service. Upon receipt of items from a mail-order business, we would deliver them immediately to the purchasers, and the SDs would collect payment upon delivery. We would then invoice the mail-order house for the fees for Takkyūbin delivery and Collect Service. Payment for goods would be collected through Friday of each week, and then paid as an aggregate into our client's account every Wednesday. In other words, the payments collected by our SDs at time of delivery would get back to the mail-order house within a minimum of five days, or twelve days at the most. For our clients, nothing could be more convenient.

Our fee schedule was ¥300 for items valued at ¥10,000 or less; ¥400 for items from ¥10,000 to ¥30,000; ¥600 for items between ¥30,000 and ¥100,00; and ¥1,000 for items between ¥100,000 and ¥300,000. Normally when you use a credit card the store pays the credit card company a fee of about 5 percent, so Collect Service was a better deal at only 2 to 3 percent.

The risk to Yamato Transport was close to zero, since our policy was not to hand over the goods unless we received payment. Even in cases when Yamato handed over the payments in five days, the goods had been delivered and paid for several days beforehand, so we had several days' use of interest-free funds, nothing to sneeze at, in addition to the handling fees we were already charging.

Collect Service was established as a wholly-owned subsidiary of Yamato Transport in July 1986, and has grown steadily since its launch, posting quite respectable figures. In the 1998 fiscal year, they looked like this:

- Number of shippers: 59,634
- Number of items: 32.1 million
- Sales revenue: ¥10.9 billion
- Before-tax profits: ¥2.6 billion
- Payments handled: ¥484.7 billion

Book Service

Another company established as a subsidiary of Yamato Transport is our Book Service—this time as a joint venture with Kurita Shuppan Hanbai, Co., Ltd., one of Japan's major book distributors.

The reason we set up our Book Service was because book marketing and distribution in Japan was sticking to traditional ways of doing things, and seemed, at least from the outside, to be mired in an outdated and unchanging system.

This move was also rooted in my hunch that Takkyūbin's growth would flatten out before long, and when it did, it might be necessary to take advantage of the Takkyūbin network to enter the world of retail sales.

Book distribution is a very unusual realm. First of all, each book is a unique and independent product—and 60,000 to 70,000 new titles are published every year. The book distribution industry is made up of three elements: publishers, distributors, and retailers (bookstores). The publisher releases the books, which then pass through the hands of the distributors to the retailers. The books change hands, but are neither bought nor sold; sales are on a consignment basis, and the bookstores are free to return any unsold books to the publisher after a month or two.

It is this consignment system I was referring to when I spoke of the book distribution system as being outdated. However, without it, books with limited popular appeal, such as those of a scholarly or specialized nature, would never reach their readers, so if you think about it, the system is actually a good one, grounded in practical wisdom. On the other hand, when you go to a bookstore you can always find the best-sellers, but if you want a book that is not in stock, ordering it will commonly take as long as a month.

So we envisioned a book service that would allow you to place an order for a book over the phone or via fax, and have it delivered by Takkyūbin in less than a week. While incredibly convenient for the reader, this concept threatened the very livelihood of the bookstores. Nor was it something the distributors would be likely to go along with, either.

In the world of book marketing, the power of the distributors is absolute—even the major publishers defer to them. We were told that if we launched our Book Service, strong united opposition from the bookstores and the distributors could make even the publishing companies themselves hesitate to provide us with books.

So we approached Kurita Shuppan Hanbai, one of the biggest distributors, with an offer of a joint venture, hoping to enlist their aid. Kurita's president, keenly aware of the coming wave of modernization in the distribution industry, was kind enough to agree to our offer.

Once we had created the company, I wanted to begin test-marketing immediately, though I was also afraid that if we failed at that stage, we might never get the project up and running again. So we located the company headquarters in Okayama Prefecture, and quietly began test-marketing. Why Okayama? Because it was far from Tokyo and had the reputation of being a prefecture that was enthusiastic about education.

The distributors were scary enough, but I was also worried about the response of the bookstores. I knew that Nisshoren, the nationwide booksellers association, had an annual New Year's convention in Tokyo. Important issues, such as the raising of margins, were discussed at the general assembly meetings during this convention. News of the establishment of our Okayama book service was reported to the general assembly and I was concerned that if it passed a protest resolution, we'd be back at square one. I held my breath throughout the proceedings, but was relieved to find out that though the news had aroused a certain amount of comment, no protest was forthcoming. The following year we moved the headquarters of the Book Service to Tokyo, and began a vigorous sales campaign.

The Book Service works like this. You place an order by phone, fax, the Internet, or by any other means—and four days to a week later the book you ordered is delivered to your doorstep by Takkyūbin. The cost: the price of the book(s) plus ¥362—no matter how many books you order.

In the beginning, the Book Service was not exactly a household word, and we did not find that many users. But as time went by, people began to realize how convenient it was, and our user base gradually expanded. It was especially welcomed by people living in areas where there were few bookstores, and our network of repeat customers grew. We also gave special discounts to community centers and public libraries in remote areas. More and more publishers began to entrust fulfillment of their direct orders to the Book Service. And some of the big regional bookstores began to look to us to fulfill orders from their customers for books that they did not have in stock. When bookstores ordered from the distributors, it might be a month before they saw the book. But if they ordered through the Book Service, the book would be in their customer's hands in about a week.

I wasn't aware of it before getting involved in the mail-order book trade, but book distribution is a strange and difficult business. First of all, you'd be surprised at how often publishers are out of stock of their own books when you try to order them. They don't print that many copies of the first edition of your average book—in most cases, fewer copies than there are bookstores nationwide. And since it is a consignment system, the majority of the copies that have been printed are in circulation, not sitting in the publisher's inventory. Therefore, when the Book Service receives an order, it frequently takes a bit of work to locate a copy of the book. Our goal is to do this within six days, and we manage this about 95 percent of the time, but it can sometimes take as long as ten days to fill some of our orders.

The antiquated nature of the distribution system has actually led to appreciation for the existence of the Book Service. And the result—particularly as the Internet has come into ever more widespread use—has been a steady increase in orders.

In 1998, the numbers looked like this:

- Number of orders: 747,000
- Number of books ordered: 1.86 million
- Value of books: ¥3.1 billion
- Shipping and handling fees: ¥154 million

In addition, the Book Service uses Yamato's Collect Service to collect payments for the books and the shipping and handling charges. There's no risk involved, and the two augment each other's income.

Internet use is likely to keep growing by leaps and bounds. In an information society, all barriers are down; and as a result, I confidently predict a new era for venture businesses is on the horizon. But even as information flows through new channels, goods are not going to suddenly fly through the air on their own. Because of this, the demand for Takkyūbin will definitely continue to grow, as will the demand for ancillary services related to Takkyūbin.

I've been told many times that sooner or later, Takkyūbin will peak. But it seems certain that at this very moment an almost unimaginable, unprecedented new demand is in the process of being created. And when it is, the Takkyūbin network that has been extended to cover 100 percent of Japan's area will have yet another chance to demonstrate its enormous power.

Strengthening the Financial Profile

I n the twenty years or so since we launched Takkyūbin, Yamato Transport's capitalization has increased more than a hundredfold. Here I'd like to speak a bit about what we have done over the years to improve our financial position.

Before we launched Takkyūbin, Yamato Transport was dependent on bank loans for financing. However, by equity- and debt-financing and cash revenues from the Takkyūbin operations, we were gradually able to decrease our borrowing. In addition, by issuing convertible and foreign currency bonds, we diversified our access to sources of funds.

As our operations continued to grow, our stock price kept rising to new highs. This made financing easier, which allowed us to engage in more capital investment to strengthen the company's competitiveness, which led to higher profits—and a "virtuous circle" was born. The high quality of our service had become our financial underpinning.

The Situation Prior to Takkyūbin

My father and predecessor as president of Yamato, Ogura Yasuomi, had a keen business sense, but finance and accounting were not his strong suit. This is generally true of founders of companies.

Japanese companies rarely start out as large, heavily capitalized operations—nearly all of them began as small private firms. Yamato Transport was founded in 1919 as a joint-stock company capitalized at ¥100,000, but

Note: A table of yen-doller exchange rates can be found at the front of the book.

that was for show—in reality it was nothing more than a small, privately held company.

By May 1944, toward the end of World War II, Yamato's capital stood at only ¥1,845,000, which you would have to call undercapitalized for a trucking company with a fleet of 330 trucks.

Moreover, in accordance with the wartime policy of the Railroad Ministry (at the time there was no Ministry of Transport, and the Railroad Ministry was responsible for regulating trucking as well), Yamato was absorbed by Nippon Express, which was given control of all our stock. After the war, in September 1947, we were able to buy all our stock back from Nippon Express, and increase our capitalization to ¥5 million.

But our problems began there. We were organized as a modern joint-stock company, but in reality were operating as a privately held firm, and because of this, we did not have sufficient funds to double our capitalization. So through our brokerage firm we sought introduction to a private investor. This was a very wealthy man who had a huge mansion in Nakano Ward in Tokyo looking out over about an acre of lawn and gardens, and who was a major shareholder in several private railways in the Kantō region and in a major entertainment company. He was a conservative investor, who liked to hold onto his stock long-term and collect his dividends, rather than playing the market.

It turned out he was also a member of the same golf club as my father, and they soon reached a meeting of minds: the investor promised to chip in his money but stay out of the running of the business. The problem was that he had purchased about 40 percent of Yamato's stock! The fact that a single investor was holding 40 percent of our stock became a real headache for us when we tried to raise capital later on. This guy was wealthy, but since he never traded stock, his income was almost entirely from dividends. So when Yamato wanted to issue more stock to increase its capitalization and needed substantial funds to do so, we still had to scramble for financing.

My father later admitted that this had been a mistake—but I was the one who had to struggle for twenty-six years to correct it.

I'm no financial genius, either. Learning from the errors of my father, who you might call tone-deaf as far as finance was concerned, I have tended to leave the details to professional financial consultants we've hired. But I have also made an effort to understand and stay on top of the big picture. And I think it's fortunate that my head wasn't turned by the various financial shenanigans of Japan's bubble era.

The trucking business requires a lot of capital investment. The main reason Yamato slipped into being a C class company during Japan's high-growth era was our slowness to enter the long-distance trucking business; but at the base of this was our undercapitalization, and the effects of inadequate investment in plant and equipment.

As a result of ten capital increases by means of shareholders' allotment, our capitalization jumped from ¥5 million in 1947 to ¥500 million in 1971, but we were always struggling with the burden of undercapitalization. As a result, we had to rely on bank loans for financing—and we borrowed from every bank we could. The only thing that kept us from collapsing under the weight of all this debt was our principal bank, which gave me a deep appreciation for how important it is in Japan to have such a relationship with a financial institution.

We reached a turning point in our financial situation in 1974 when we increased our capitalization from ¥500 million to ¥800 million. This was a result of releasing a million out of our six million shares for a public offering at the current stock price. A number of times before we had wanted to engage in equity financing through such a public offering of new shares at market value, and had spoken to our biggest stockholder about it, but he scoffed at the idea, saying he would not go along with anything that would dilute the ratio of his stock. He did not know that there were ways to raise capital other than a rights offering to shareholders, but after years of effort, we finally got it through his thick head. If we could just get him to agree to the idea of a public offering of new shares, it might take years, but given enough time we could gradually reduce the percentage of our stock that he held, and the future would look somewhat brighter.

I can still remember the day that we got the OK from his office to go ahead with the public offering. It was about three o'clock in the afternoon. It happened to be during one of the sumo tournaments, and our shareholder personally held one of the coveted box seats at the Kokugikan. He said to me, "I haven't given today's tickets to anyone yet, so why don't you take them?" I thanked him, and headed off to the stadium. By the time I got there, it was nearing the end of the day's main matches. I don't remember who was wrestling, but I will never forget the feeling of lolling around all by myself in that private box, watching the sumo.

Diversifying Funding

When we launched Takkyūbin, Yamato Transport's capitalization stood at ¥840 million.

We immediately needed to make a series of major capital investments in constructing bases across the country, deploying delivery vans, and so on. In fiscal 1976 we invested a total of about ¥2.5 billion in plant and equipment; in 1980 this figure rose to ¥5.3 billion, and from 1981 onward it was beginning to exceed ¥10 billion.

Replenishing our capital stock had become a very urgent matter.

The method we had found for doing this was the public stock issues at market price I mentioned above. Between 1977 and 1982 we made five such offerings, raising ¥14.3 billion in capital.

Moreover, Takkyūbin revenues were in cash, so we no longer had to increase our borrowing from the banks—in fact, from 1977 onward, we began to pay down our debt to the financial institutions.

As another means of increasing funds, we began public offerings of convertible bonds. Between 1982 and 1986 we carried out four such issues, raising ¥70 billion. At the time of their issue, convertible bonds are a debt obligation requiring the payment of interest, but which can be exchanged for a specified number of shares of common stock when a predetermined conversion price is reached. In other words, they have the interesting ability to convert from a liability into capital. When they are converted to shares, the company must pay dividends on them, but no longer has the obligation to repay them as debt, so from the point of view of management, they are a useful way of strengthening the company's financial standing.

However, the prerequisite for conversion from bond into stock is that the stock price must rise to the predetermined conversion price, so the company has to keep working to turn a profit—a pressure which can be seen in a positive light. But there is a danger that if the stock price stalls below the conversion price, the conversion cannot take place, and when the bond reaches maturity it will have to be redeemed. Fortunately, Yamato has never had to worry about having to do this.

Issuing bonds outside Japan was another major contribution to beefing up our finances. The advantage of foreign-cuurency denominated bonds was that the regulations regarding their issue were a bit looser, and the interest rates were lower. In June 1983 we issued our first convertible bonds denominated in Swiss francs. A total of four such issues raised us about ¥49.1 billion.

As a result of all these efforts at diversifying funding, we have been able to spend nearly ¥40 billion a year on investment in plant and equipment, establishing seventy bases across the country (more than one per prefecture) and creating the facilities that have served as the backbone of our nationwide network.

Freight transport is a labor-intensive industry. The need for investment in plant and equipment is probably limited compared to manufacturing. This is particularly true of chartered truck-load carriers. The principal assets are the trucks, whose serviceable life is about four years for big rigs and three for smaller trucks, and which can be purchased on the installment system. If you are an LTL carrier, you will also have to put money into building a few large freight terminals.

So if you think about it, Takkyūbin was an exception. It required setting up a network on a nationwide scale, which required an enormous amount of capital. Cool Takkyūbin meant spending even more on refrigerators and other specialized equipment. The only thing that made it possible to implement a financial strategy that could take care of this kind of expenditure was the gift of the "virtuous cycle."

When I recall the undercapitalization we struggled with before we started Takkyūbin—total capital of only ¥800 million—it seems like a different world. At the end of March 1999 our capitalization stood at more than ¥101.5 billion. Our total investment in plant and equipment for the 1998 fiscal year reached ¥40 billion, largely for land (¥9.5 billion), buildings (¥9.5 billion), and trucks (¥10 billion). In the same year we invested about ¥5 billion in Cool Takkyūbin, bringing our cumulative expenditure on it since its inception in April 1988 to a total of ¥45 billion.

The reason we were able to engage in all this capital investment was because Takkyūbin was doing so well, and the value of our stock kept continually rising. Because we were able to maintain the stock price at a high level, it became easier to raise funds, and plentiful working capital could be used to introduce new plant and equipment and increase the efficiency of our operations. Increased efficiency cut costs, raised our competitiveness, and increased our revenues. In short, we had created a mechanism for increasing income and profits—a "virtuous circle" was born.

What was the starting point of this "virtuous circle"? In Yamato's case it was the high quality of our service. This excellent service was a product of the enthusiastic efforts of our sales drivers in the field. The result was that we gradually developed a bit of financial leeway, and were able to make capital investments that improved the work environment and helped complete the development of our nationwide network. We began with humanware, improved our hardware, and completed the cycle by finalizing our software system.

It is easy to think about finance as something distinct from operations, but it is not—the two are intimately related.

A Cash Business

Before Takkyūbin, Yamato Transport was primarily a commercial freight carrier. So it did not seem strange that it took us so much time to get paid.

The fastest arrangement by which we were paid for our services was a monthly billing cycle, payable the following month. And it was standard with our larger clients that this payment was not in cash but in the form of a promissory note. The period of the notes varied with the client, but in the worst cases it might be anywhere from 120 to 150 days.

Being a labor-intensive industry, more than 50 percent of operating expenses in the trucking trade is for personnel costs—and due to the payment schedules I have just described, there were months when our short-term cash flow and financing were so bad that we had to struggle just to make payroll.

But when we launched Takkyūbin, cash started to flow in on a daily basis. This was amazing! It is embarrassing to admit that I did not realize the implications of this until after we commenced our Takkyūbin operations, but I honestly had not thought of it before. The year of the launch, 1976, we handled 1.7 million parcels, which meant that we were pulling in an average of ¥2 million a day in cash revenue.

The contribution this daily cash income made to our financial position was incredible. In the 1998 fiscal year our income from Takkyūbin was a bit more than ¥560 billion, which meant that our daily cash revenue averaged about ¥1.5 billion. As a result, we were able to hold long- and short-term loans to ¥11 billion out of Yamato's total liabilities of ¥264.5 billion, and interest-bearing liabilities as a whole to ¥158.2 billion—which meant that Yamato had come to the point where it could be counted among the blue-chip companies in terms of its financials. Only after starting Takkyūbin did I develop such a deep appreciation for what having a daily source of cash income can do for a company. What other businesses are so blessed? Not manufacturing. On the other hand, it is far from rare in the world of retail and the service industries.

Daily cash revenue not only makes it easier to generate working capital, it has many other positive effects, such as providing more latitude for innovation in business. For example, it is the fact that they are a cash business that allows retail stores to have post-season sales in order to clear inventory. The same is true of the airlines and the deep discounts they give on unfilled seats. You could also say that the reason Yamato was able to start its Collect Service aimed at mail-order businesses was because our core Takkyūbin operation was bringing in so much cash.

However, if cash income makes you greedy for more, and you go chasing after high-risk financial instruments such as derivatives, it can lead to real problems. Yamato Transport did not go down that road, so we have been able to enjoy only the up side of our cash revenues.

PART THREE

My Philosophy of Management

After World War II, the industries supporting the Japanese economy were transformed, one after the other. First textiles, then steel, shipbuilding, consumer electronics, and automobiles flourished; and the top firms in each of these fields led both the domestic economy and Japan's export trade. Yet with the passage of time, all of them were swept over by the waves of corporate restructuring. Rise and fall—it's the way of the world. A tactical response to the immediate situation is important, but it goes without saying that you must develop a long-term strategic outlook.

Management is a logical accumulation. Poor managers simply imitate the successes of other companies. What is essential is to think through the logic behind the success of others, and understand how to apply it to your own company. If you don't have the ability to think things through in this way, you are not really a manager.

A corporation is a social entity. Not only does it contribute to society by the creation of wealth and services, it also provides employment opportunities. To do this, a company must achieve continuity. And continuity requires an ethically grounded, upstanding corporate character.

Ethics means taking a consistently fair approach to all business relations—with clients and customers, suppliers, shareholders, employees. Top management must always be fair, setting an example for the employees.

Organizational Vitality

The worst flaw in Japanese organizations is their rigid seniority systems. These systems create pyramidal hierarchies and block the introduction of merit-based systems of management. If you can flatten the corporate pyramid and improve internal communication, management becomes more nimble.

On the other hand, establishing a fair and accurate system for personnel evaluation is an extremely difficult proposition. In my efforts to do so, I have made a point of incorporating "bottom up" and "horizontal" evaluations from subordinates and peers, and have tried to evaluate the overall character of each employee.

As a company grows, it has a tendency to become organizationally top-heavy and bureaucratized. Managers must constantly be on guard against such corporate bloat, and search for ways to maintain the vitality of their organization.

Postwar Organizational Theory—The Line and Staff System

Postwar Japan struggled heroically to rebuild an industrial base that had been devastated by the war. Factories rose out of the ashes, and production resumed.

The leader of Japan's recovery was secondary industry—manufacturing. With America as the benchmark, and "catch up and surpass" as the slogan, productivity gradually increased. Management seminars were held all over the country, introducing the latest in management theory. As I mentioned in chapter 2, I attended a number of them and learned a great deal. A principal theme of many of them was organizational theory, and it was there that I first heard of the line and staff system.

Like the productivity theory I learned from other seminars, line-and-staff organizational theory was all based on case studies drawn from American manufacturing. It was not necessarily appropriate to the Japanese situation, especially to management of a service-sector company like Yamato Transport; but I didn't realize that at the time, and put a lot of thought into trying to adapt it to our company.

In the line/staff system, core functions such as production and sales are defined as line operations, while administration, personnel, accounting, and other functions supporting the line operations are defined as staff operations. The point was to achieve a division of labor between these operations.

As theory, it was easy to understand and enjoyed a certain period of popularity, but it really wasn't all that useful in making management more effective. Line operations were basically the shop floors and sales offices, while staff operations belonged largely to the administrative apparatus of the main office. Because of this, there was a strong tendency for staff to see themselves as the core of management and supervision, and to order the line operations around.

This was not the original intent of this theory, which was to promote clarity of function and organizational efficiency by removing indirect administrative tasks from the front-line manufacturing and sales operations. The problem was that the staff operations responsible for these indirect administrative tasks tended to become top-heavy, place unreasonable demands for information on the line operations, and slow the process of corporate decision-making. And in any case, this organizational theory was intended for manufacturing, not service industries.

The Fad for Divisional Management

One way of thinking of organizations is in terms of units based on the content of the work in which they are engaged. Known as "divisional management," this organizational model was adopted by many companies at one time. One of the reasons it became so popular was that aggressive implementation of a divisional management framework was seen as one of the motive forces behind the success of Matsushita Electric (better known outside Japan by the brand-name Panasonic), Japan's largest home appliance and electronics manufacturer.

The basic idea behind divisional management is the creation of divisions within the company based on the type of product they are marketing. The unique feature of this system is that each of these divisions is conceived of as an independent profit center, and is entrusted with an extraordinary degree of authority that makes it, in effect, an autonomous company within the company.

In fact, it would probably make more sense just to establish these "internal companies" as independent subsidiaries, but I think one of the reasons for the popularity of the divisional management concept was the fear that to do so would run the parent company afoul of Japan's Antimonopoly Law.

The divisional management model had one advantage over the creation of independent subsidiaries, and that lay in the fact that financing and management were conducted in a unified manner from the main office. However, this was back in the days when many companies depended on loans from financial institutions for the bulk of their funding. If an operation is strong enough to be spun off as a separate company that can be listed independently on the stock exchange, then that approach is even more advantageous.

In any case, since the provisions of the Antimonopoly Law have now been substantially loosened, permitting the creation of holding companies, the situation has changed radically. Nowadays, if you want the managerial efficiency and accountability that was the goal of creating divisions based on product lines, you'd be better off simply setting up separate subsidiaries, if possible.

Of course, if you are just starting a new operation, it may need a long incubation period before it is ready to stand on its own, and in that case the divisional idea has its merits. Chief among these is the fact that as a division, the new operation will still be integrated into the accounting system of the parent company, allowing for various financial adjustments to support it. However, in the current climate of full corporate disclosure, financials must be made available not just for the company as a whole but for product lines and divisions as well. Which brings me back to the idea that setting up independent subsidiaries right from the beginning is probably the best bet for establishing a long-term strategy.

The Individual Depreciation System

This approach looks at organizations from a slightly different angle: the individual, who comprises the smallest unit of the company.

It is not a term familiar to most people, but in the transport industry, there are companies making use of a system called individual depreciation. This began with taxi companies, and then enjoyed a certain amount of popularity with trucking companies. In simple terms, it is a system that involves the creation of individual employee-run enterprises within the larger company.

In the taxi and trucking industries, the vehicles are normally corporate property. In the individual depreciation system, the vehicles are owned by the company on paper, but are in fact operated as the property of individual employees.

Why do this? Because if the vehicle is not owned by a corporate entity, it is impossible to secure operating permits and licenses. At present, under the Road Transportation Law, taxis are not allowed to operate without a license. Trucking has been deregulated, and the old Trucking Business Law has been replaced by a permission system, but the fact of the matter is that you still must secure permission to operate a trucking business. Private taxis are permitted, but the requirements are strict and not everyone can obtain a license. The individual operation of a truck as a business enterprise is not even permitted by law.

This situation is what gave birth to the individual depreciation system, in which vehicles are legally owned by the company, but are in fact given to individual employees to operate and manage. Strictly speaking, of course, this is against the law.

Here's how it works. First the company withholds a management fee of 30 to 40 percent of the monthly gross of each vehicle (taking it out of the gross is the beauty part). Then it deducts cost of depreciation, fuel, and maintenance. What's left becomes the driver's salary. When the depreciation period has come to an end and the vehicle is replaced, any profit on the difference between its sale price and the book value becomes the driver's.

The driver works to increase daily revenues, cares for the vehicle, does his best to avoid accidents, and tries to keep fuel and maintenance costs down. In some cases, drivers even take their vehicles home with them—saving the company from having to garage them. The company secures a stable source of revenue, and the drivers, if they put in the effort, are rewarded by seeing their own incomes increase. It's a system in which both employer and employee benefit, but because it infringes upon both the Road Transportation Law and the Labor Standards Law, no one publicly admits to using it. It is rumored to be in pretty widespread use, however, especially in the Osaka area.

It would be nice if trucks, like taxis, were permitted to be operated by individuals. That's an issue of transportation policy, but since private taxis are permitted, I don't see any reason why the restrictions on trucks couldn't simply be eliminated.

In manufacturing there is an organized system of subcontracting, often several layers deep, with small work teams called *kumi* at the very bottom. "Outsourcing" has also become a buzzword lately, and in many cases the basic unit of organization is the individual. It seems to me that to make these sort of systems work, you need to think of them not in terms of organizational theory, but in terms of communication.

Flattening the Pyramid

There is an inherent problem common to all organizations, and that is the inevitable tendency to self-propagation and bloat known as Parkinson's Law.

Since organizations are premised on the division of labor, certain units come into being that have no direct relationship to the original purposes of the organization. Known as indirect departments, they frequently add staff and grow bloated over time.

Once an organization has come into being, the communication and coordination work involved in maintaining it keeps on growing. In a large corporation you must stay alert for signs of bureaucratization.

In Japanese organizations something that requires particular attention is the custom of determining everything by seniority. In Japan we often think of promotions and job assignments primarily in terms of seniority, and this leads to major problems. In recent years many people have finally begun to call for a merit-based system, but the seniority system is its polar opposite—and is preventing the adoption of merit-based approaches.

A merit-based approach requires the ability to select young talent to fill positions with the most capable and best-suited personnel. This means promoting them over the heads of people senior to them, but if you let worries about side effects such as friction between employees stop you, you can't do this. And what you wind up with is a safe and predictable escalator system of promotion.

One practical problem with the seniority system is that in many cases it increases the number of executive positions in the company. You often hear stories like the company that promoted most of the managers in the same age group to the rank of vice-president and then dealt with the rest by making them deputy vice-presidents! Promotion based on seniority is intimately related to pyramidal organization. The organizational pyramid provides the stages that the employees ascend step by step when their time comes.

Clerk, supervisor, head supervisor, deputy section manager, section or branch manager, deputy vice-president, vice-president—the employee gradually ascends the ladder. So in order to abandon the seniority system, you first have to collapse the organizational pyramid. And if you flatten the organization, then it becomes impossible to adopt a seniority system even if you wanted to. If the only executive positions you have are vice-president and manager, then there is no way to fill them other than merit-based selection.

The aim in simplifying the organizational structure is to move the profit centers of the corporation as close to the front lines as possible. And to do this you need to delegate responsibility to the shop floor.

Flattening the organization means devolving responsibility for profit closer to the front lines. Doing this not only improves corporate communication and makes management more nimble—it also motivates the frontline employees. Flat organization is particularly desirable in the service industries and in retail.

Japanese companies are known for the high morale and productivity of their employees. While this is true of blue-collar workers, white-collar workers are notoriously inefficient. And I believe that this is because employers and employees alike are stuck in the seniority system. But I don't think Japanese companies will have the luxury of being stuck there for very much longer.

Employee Evaluations

A corporation might be defined as an organization uniting a large number of employees in a collaborative effort to achieve common goals. The organization itself is created in order to achieve those goals effectively. Yet no matter how well-structured the corporation may be, if the employees lack motivation, good results will not be forthcoming.

This is why we have company rules, systems of compensation, and human resources management. And in order to ensure that all these function properly, you need personnel evaluations based on actual performance.

When I joined Yamato Transport, my first assignment was to the labor section of the personnel department. When I was sent to our subsidiary in Shizuoka, I went as general manager, so you might say I cut my teeth in the personnel and labor relations field. To be frank, sales was never my strong suit, and I always felt more at home with managing matters such as working hours and wages. Yet the one thing I was unable to achieve in my forty-two years at Yamato Transport was the creation of a really satisfactory system for employee evaluations.

Employee evaluations are terribly important. Employees work hard because they want the value of their work to be appreciated. And if you want to bring vitality to your organization, then fair evaluations of their work, reflected in promotions and raises, are essential. However, when it comes to the methodology for accomplishing this, you quickly run into difficulties. This is because in Japan few employees work alone; almost everything is done by groups.

If you want to conduct accurate, performance-based employee evaluations, you have to start with an analysis of what each employee is doing on the job. But this is difficult. For example—though this has changed for the better in recent years—female employees used to get stuck with miscellaneous tasks like pouring tea and making copies, and it was difficult to assess the time they spent on actually doing their work.

Another approach is to make the field office the unit for evaluating performance, but here you run into a wall as well. Just as an example, say the last head of the office was really doing a fine job, and that one of the results of that is that high performance continues under his successor—pretty difficult to evaluate who is responsible, isn't it?

Then there is always the problem of individual differences among the people conducting the evaluations. Some managers go too hard on employees in evaluations, others too soft. You can imagine the range. There are probably managers who will give all their staff pretty much the same rating; others who will give both extremely good and extremely bad ratings. At one point I researched and implemented a system invented by a famous compensation analyst for correcting for such bias, but was never convinced it really worked.

My conclusion was that you couldn't depend on the views of an employee's superior. Yet for the employees, it was unacceptable to have a system in which you got the same evaluation whether you did your work properly or not. If you couldn't make a distinction between hard workers and slackers, the fairness of the system might be called into question, and disrupt the whole fabric of the company.

So what I came up with was "bottom up" evaluations by subordinates and "horizontal" evaluations by peers. And the content of these evaluations was not performance, but "character."

Is he or she honest? Straightforward? Unselfish and helpful to others? Compassionate? On the evaluations, character traits such as these were to be rated. Like multiple judges at an athletic event, the ratings of the various subordinates and peers could be assembled and averaged. In other words, the evaluation was based on a number of different viewpoints.

In Japan it is difficult to find an objective standard that can be applied to performance evaluations. So if this is the case, the next best thing seemed to be to try these "evaluations from below." Not as the sole criterion for evaluation, or course, but in tandem with other systems—for I believe that when all is said and done, an employee of good character will be a good employee who will make the customers happy.

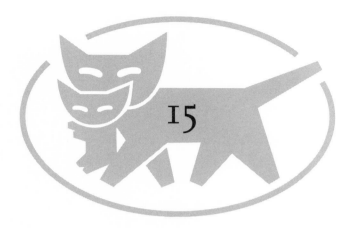

Ten Requirements for the Business Leader

I n closing, I want to talk about what it takes to be a business leader. To my mind, logical thinking and high ethical standards are indispensable to a businessman.

Management is a process of continuous logical decisions, and people who are incapable of logical thought are not qualified to be managers.

A true business leader must possess an independent spirit. A surprising number of business executives have been content to travel in convoy under the protection of bureaucrats and politicians. But we are rapidly becoming a borderless society, faced with competitors we may not even know about. A proactive, logically guided stance is essential.

So is a strong sense of ethics. Employees are always watching their boss. If the top man in the organization sets an example with his own behavior, I am convinced that the ethics of the entire company will be strengthened.

1. Logical Thinking

The most important requirement for being a business leader is the ability to think in a logical manner. This is because management itself is a process of logical assessments.

Management requires planning for a variety of eventualities. Making those plans requires making predictions about the future. Whether those predictions are hits or misses is the true test of an entrepreneur.

You start with certain givens, predicate certain variables, determine goals, and set the wheels in motion. Whether or not you achieve the results you expected depends on the depth of your skill at reading the situation.

The depth of that skill is determined by how much thought you have given to the variables. If you consider as many as possible, and if you weigh them accurately, correct predictions are possible. The reason they are frequently mistaken is the human factor, which always contains unpredictable elements.

The human mind is constantly in motion, and difficult to read from outside. Moreover, in different times and places people reveal different aspects of their personality. People have their preferences, but these are also swayed by the trends of the times; anxiety about the future often makes people change their minds.

But the kind of prediction required in business management is not really that difficult. If you are prepared to work by trial and error, and change variables not just in the planning stage but also during implementation of a plan, making minor adjustments and calculating their effect, then you can probably predict outcomes without being too far off the mark. In fact, the trial-and-error process is quite valuable.

But for really important decisions, the predictions you make in the planning stage are critical. And at such times you want to make sure to do your homework.

When we launched Takkyūbin, most people predicted we would fail. But those predictions were based on awfully shallow grounds—nothing much more than a guess that such an inefficient line of work was likely to drive us into the red.

In trying to assess the profitability of Takkyūbin, figuring costs was not so difficult—many of them were fixed, and basically what it boiled down to was how much we would have to spend per day per truck. The question was revenues. Unit price was pegged to the price of the postal service's small parcel service, so we couldn't charge more than ¥500. What we needed to know was how many parcels we would be handling a day. In other words, the "density" of our freight was crucial. Demand was probably a function of population. The operational efficiency of our vans would vary with the size of their assigned areas. Given these factors, it was inevitable that we would lose money the first few years, but after a while we would probably cross the threshold into profitability. . . . I don't think many people, when predicting Takkyūbin's success or failure, thought things through to this extent. Then, five years later, when Takkyūbin began running in the black, thirty companies suddenly wanted a piece of the action—also without any real consideration of what we had done to make this happen.

To make a long story short, I think the people who make the most dangerous business executives are those who don't think for themselves and simply imitate what others are doing. The opposite of logic is emotion. People who only think emotionally are not suited to be executives.

People who are logical thinkers can give you a coherent account of how they arrived at their conclusions. In giving such an account, they may at times be giving logical shape to their own thoughts. The ability to explain things effectively to other people is an important requirement for being a business leader.

2. Reading the Trends of the Times

Corporations are social entities. As such, they are strongly influenced by the winds of social change. The executive must be able to accurately read which way the wind is blowing. Takkyūbin's success came in part because the trends of the times provided Yamato Transport with a strong following wind.

When you look back on postwar Japan, it is clear that with just about every decade there was a change in the social and economic climate.

The decade from 1945 to 1955 was a struggle with hunger. Supplies were short, and each day brought a continual effort to put food on the table. The driving force in that period was primary industry—farmers and fisher men. People sold their heirloom kimonos to the farmers for food.

From 1955 to 1965, secondary industry—manufacturing—led Japan's recovery from the war. The key word was productivity.

From 1965 to 1975, tertiary industry—distribution—led the economy. The distribution revolution linked mass production with mass marketing via volume distribution. Consumer durables became more affordable, and Japanese households more affluent.

1975 to 1985 has been called the age of the consumer. Consumers drove the economy. Marketing was taken very seriously in an effort to determine consumer preferences, and new high-tech products flooded the market.

1985 to 1995 was the "lifestyle" decade. In an atmosphere of material abundance, people sought a more relaxed and comfortable mode of living. New culture and leisure industries boomed. Takkyūbin caught the wave of this era, and flourished.

And the present? The present is the "borderless" era. In terms of the economy, national borders have disappeared. But the boundaries have also fallen between government and private sector, national and local, men and women, day and night. The focus is on the individual as the basic unit of life and economic activity. Telephones are no longer shared by a household, but carried by individuals. And with the rapid diffusion of personal computers and the Internet, the information system has changed completely.

These days, one's competition is not necessarily limited to companies in the same industry. We've hit a point where competitors can arise from places we haven't even dreamed of. The business leader has to be able to read the currents of the times with sensitivity. Right now, he must be mentally prepared to adapt to the challenges of a borderless world.

3. Strategic Thinking

In management there is strategy, and then there is tactics. Tactics are the plans for defeating the competition in the arena of everyday business activity; strategy is long-range planning to achieve managerial goals.

Business executives cannot allow themselves to get stuck at the tactical level. They must always be ready to approach a situation from the strategic point of view.

Executives who label everything top priority and whip their staff into a frenzy over every issue are people who can only think tactically. At a meeting on competition with rival firms they will shout "Market share first! Sales first!," but when the end of the quarter comes around it will be "Profits first!" and at other times it will be "Environment first!" or "Safety first!" or whatever.

People like this are not qualified to be executives. The role of the executive is precisely to determine the company's priorities and communicate them to its employees. The priority at any given time may not be sales or profits; it could be the environment, or product quality.

Years ago, one of Yamato's subsidiaries was not being managed very well, discipline went slack, and there were a lot of accidents. We had to do something about this, and so we put out the slogan "Safety first, business second," and engaged in a thorough campaign of accident prevention. As a result, not only were there fewer accidents, but operating costs as a whole went down and the bottom line improved

Strategic thinking is also what imparts a kind of dynamic to management. If you are going to insist that something is number one, it's a good idea to establish a number two.

All things have their merits and demerits. If you reduce staff you reduce personnel costs, but you also reduce your labor power. If you add employees, you gain labor power, but you also incur greater personnel costs. To

decide which is appropriate at any given time requires considerable strategic judgment.

Again, if you want to provide the best service to your customers, you
will incur costs. Conversely, if you hold costs down, you know service will
suffer. Which will you choose? Service and costs are a trade-off. Which one
you favor will have a major impact on your business. Management is basically a series of such trade-offs. The sort of strategic decisions that only a
top executive can make are constantly being demanded of you.

4. Proactive Management

From now on, corporate management must be prepared to be exposed to
increasingly intense competition. In a borderless world, you cannot predict
when a new competitor may appear on the scene.

In management, a proactive stance is crucial. Defensive management
simply means dying by inches.

The classic example of defensive management is what I call "convoy-
style management." The businessman primarily interested in safety may
see nothing wrong with it, and sail along without a care in the world—until he realizes one day that the entire convoy has fallen hopelessly behind.

For many years the Tokyo–Hokkaidō air route was divided among three
long-established airlines. There was a lot of passenger traffic, and the route
was regarded as something of a cash cow. The three airlines were secure in
charging high fares until one day a new competitor appeared, touching off
a price war that ended up cutting the standard fare in half.

But the problem had existed before the new competitor even came
on the scene. It was just that the three existing airlines hadn't noticed it.
And that was the fact that for some time tourists had been avoiding the
high Hokkaidō fares and taking their vacations where cheap flights were
available—Guam or Korea or Hong Kong. The competition was not
between the three Japanese airlines, but between these three firms and
foreign airlines and travel agencies. What they should have done was
abandon their convoy-style price-fixing and have some appropriate competition over fares, which would have won them many more customers and
actually stabilized their businesses. The fact that they were caught up in a
fare-cutting panic with no time to prepare themselves for it was a sign of
their lack of strategic thinking.

The essence of proactive management is the creation of demand.
Demand is not something that simply exists; it is made. For quite a while
people have been saying that Takkyūbin will plateau out. But year after

year it keeps growing. This is because we have not hesitated to put our efforts into developing new products and revitalizing existing services.

What is demanded of today's business leaders, now more than ever, is the entrepreneurial spirit. A company may get bigger with each passing year, but it also grows older. The true business leader must maintain an entrepreneurial spirit regardless of whether his company is new or old. When he shifts from a proactive to a defensive stance, it is time for him to pass the baton on to the next generation of managers.

Once upon a time there was an elderly and famous entrepreneur who claimed that as soon as anyone appeared who could do his job better, he would hand it over to them. But this was nonsense—he'd done nothing to groom any successor, and could not see that in fact he was blocking their path. Everyone has an ego. But the true business leader should be prepared to step aside when the time comes—even if he still feels he has the strength to do the job.

5. A Self-Reliant Spirit, Independent from the Bureaucracy

I've touched on this already, but the history of Takkyūbin has been one of struggles with the government bureaucracy.

When the confusion of the immediate postwar period had settled down, and Japan was launched on the road to recovery, there was a time when administrative guidance by government bureaucrats proved effective in the allocation of scarce resources. At that time, the bureaucrats prided themselves on being the people who were guiding Japanese society and the economy along the proper path. And I have to admit that they did leave a record of significant achievement.

But when Japan entered its period of high economic growth, the existence of the bureaucrats became, if anything, an obstacle. They were unable to outgrow the legacy of the postwar economic controls, tending to forget that Japan was a capitalist society and wanting to revert to a planned economy. Isolated in their offices in Kasumigaseki, they lost touch with the rapid changes that were sweeping the economy and society. They have a lot to answer for. With people who didn't have a clue as to the real state of the economy indulging in "administrative guidance," it was bound to be a disaster. These little emperors not only had no clothes, their power made them impossible to deal with.

I believe that government officials exist to serve the interests of the people. Because of this, when our applications for licenses to extend the Takkyūbin network were refused in order to protect established business interests, I was profoundly angered.

In the name of balancing supply and demand, the decision on whether or not to approve a license has been left to the discretion of the bureaucrats. But when you ask them about supply and demand, they don't have a single scrap of data. The authority to issue licenses and approvals, intended only as a method of administrative guidance, has been transformed into an end in itself, and the grip of the bureaucrats on this lever of power has a kind of pathetic intensity.

Of course not all of them are like this, but I am told some people become civil servants because they are attracted by the exercise of power. A pretty shabby notion.

Some business leaders do not seem to be uncomfortable following the lead of such officials. They like traveling in a government-piloted convoy because they think it maintains order in the industry and stability in business. When I hear things like this I am filled with disgust.

In 1994 the Administrative Procedures Act was passed. This law basically bans administrative guidance in the form of oral instructions. However, a fierce backlash by the bureaucrats resulted in the restriction of this provision to cases in which the parties receiving the administrative guidance request that it be put in writing. Of course this would be fine if these parties—private sector companies—always made such a request. But most of them are too timid to do so, and accept verbal guidance. The bureaucrats are a problem, but there is also a problem with the attitude of private sector executives.

The biggest problem with bureaucrats is the fact that they won't take responsibility for their actions. Everybody makes mistakes. I have made many in my career as a manager. But when I have become aware of them, I have openly apologized to my employees and have moved to correct my errors. Because of this, I have won the trust of my employees.

In Kasumigaseki I hear they like to use the word "infallibility," and I have a tough time understanding such an arrogant mentality. But what it all boils down to in the end is the fact that it is the businessman's own fault if he listens to what these clueless bureaucrats tell him.

6. Don't Depend on Politicians—Self-Help is the Only Answer

Politicians have a totally different presence in Tokyo and at the local level. In Tokyo, you are scarcely aware of them, but at the local level, their presence is felt on a daily basis and in a variety of ways.

As a result, when there's a problem there's a tendency to go to Mr. Politician to get it fixed—but you'd better watch out, for this is the road to political corruption. Both the people asking for favors and the politician being asked are operating out of their own interests, and there is bound to be a quid pro quo in it somewhere along the line.

As I have related earlier, Yamato Transport endured five or six years during which our applications for route licenses to expand our nationwide network were simply ignored.

Some people at our company were of the opinion that we should appeal to politicians to put in a word for us in this frustrating process, but I never did so. Our opponents were already lobbying with politicians to put pressure on the bureaucrats, and if we asked another set of politicians to intercede for us, then what we'd wind up with was their guys and our guys cutting some sort of compromise deal. Such a half-baked resolution would have been something we'd regret for many years to come. I am glad we stuck with the straightforward approach of appealing to the courts.

I've never bought tickets to politicians' fundraisers. I didn't want to have to respond to questions at the general shareholders' meeting as to why I had favored one politician over another.

In Japan there are professional extortionists and racketeers called *sōkaiya* whose bread and butter is disrupting shareholders' meetings with pointless filibustering and other shenanigans unless they are paid off by the company. But to my mind, these meetings only come once a year, and if an individual doesn't have the endurance to stand there and take questions for five hours—or all day if need be—then they ought to give up on being a business executive. Answering shareholder questions is the biggest responsibility an executive has. Any employee who thinks they have served the company's interests by giving money to buy off the *sōkaiya* is in fact a traitor to the cause.

Everybody wants to look good. When you are running a company people are always asking you for contributions to one thing or another. And if it is a big company, and they say, "Well, you could afford such-and-such an amount," then even if you don't really feel like giving, vanity makes it hard to turn them down. But the ability to say no is another primary requirement for being a business leader.

The way you say no is important, however, and doing it in a way that does not cause unpleasant feelings is the key. It is never very pleasant to have a request turned down, but if you listen patiently to what they say and give them an honest refusal, they really can't be angry with you.

On the other hand, if the request is reasonable, and the amount well within your means, then you should have the guts to say yes then and there, without a lot of waffling and saying that you will think about it. When the entrepreneur inspires trust, the company itself is trusted.

7. Good Media Relations

There are businessmen who hate contact with the media. I was one of them myself.

I made it a point to speak to the media only at the office. But as time went by, I was increasingly pestered at home, even late in the evening, by members of the press—so-called "night raids." So I asked them not to bother me at home. But a reporter from *Nihon Keizai Shimbun* admonished me for this, and I listened to him.

What the reporter said was that top executives, especially of corporations listed on the stock exchange, should realize that they had an obligation to respond to the mass media. And they should take up that responsibility positively—refusal to do so was really out of the question.

Once I had been confronted with the fact that the president of a major corporation is a public figure and has a responsibility to speak to the mass media, I had to agree. And from that point on I worked to meet the members of the press with a positive attitude.

One thing I noticed after I began dealing with the media more positively was that it wasn't such a bad idea.

If reporters could get their story straight from the horse's mouth, they wouldn't have to make up a bunch of nonsense to fill their stories. Moreover, in order to explain things objectively to the reporters, I had to sort out what was on my own mind. And I also learned a lot of information about the industry and the business world from them.

Of course they did not always write favorable things about Yamato Transport—sometimes they touched on the minus side as well. But after we had built up a relationship of trust, I could get them to hold off writing about certain things until I had at least had a chance to comment.

The more we appeared in the mass media, the better our name recognition with the public. But the greatest effect of all was the effect that news of their company had on Yamato's employees. This had incalculable value in terms of making them proud of their work and the company they worked for.

Many businessmen hope to use the mass media as free advertising. The members of the press have pride in their work and refuse to be so easily used. But the mission of the mass media is to put new information before the people as rapidly as possible, and they will cover anything of relevance to the consumer. This sort of publicity is far more effective than any amount of paid advertising.

Advertising and publicity are two different things. The business leader should be aware that a keen sense for publicity is a requirement of his job.

8. A Cheerful Personality

Many of the most famous and successful entrepreneurs have basically had sunny dispositions. Whether your personality is cheerful or moody seems largely a matter of heredity, but I do believe it can be changed if you work at it. By nature I have a rather introverted and antisocial personality, but as a result of deliberately working at being more cheerful and outgoing, I have by and large come to be able to behave that way without too much effort, even if at times it is just a veneer.

There is positive thinking that always looks on the bright side and anticipates good results, and negative thinking that always stresses the down side of everything. Cheerful types tend toward the former, moody people toward the latter. But a business leader must always engage in positive thinking. It's no accident that so many cheerful people have been successful as entrepreneurs.

I've come into contact with a lot of businessmen in my time, but one of the ones I respect the most is the late Inayama Yoshihiro of Nippon Steel, long-time chairman of Keidanren (the Japan Federation of Economic Organizations). I got to know Mr. Inayama as a result of a mutual interest in Tokiwazu, the singing that accompanies Kabuki performances. He was always ready with a pun or joke to lighten an occasion. Our Tokiwazu group got together once a month at a traditional Japanese restaurant in Yanagibashi. Busy as he was, Mr. Inayama attended frequently, and listened to our singing. It was also a drinking party, of course, and many of us did not listen that carefully to the singing of the other members. But Mr. Inayama was different. What impressed me was that not only was he a serious listener, but that no matter how awful the singing was, he never complained. To beginners he would say, "You've got a strong voice. Keep at it and you'll be good." He always had some words of praise. It gave me a keen sense that some of us are simply bigger-hearted than others.

There was also something deeply appealing about the fact that Mr. Inayama never tried to put any distance between himself and other people, and if anything, was kinder to people of lower rank and position than himself. After he passed away, I read the book of remembrances that had been compiled in his honor, and one of them was from a caddy at a golf club where Mr. Inayama had been chairman, who said that when Sundays rolled around he always used to pray at his household shrine that he would be able to caddy for Mr. Inayama that day. I also heard that when Mr. Inayama was in his final illness, the caddy made a get-well present of a chain of a thousand origami cranes and sent it to the hospital. Mr. Inayama was not only a cheerful soul, he was humble. He taught me that one of the qualifications for business leadership is a respect for other people and an ability to see and to appreciate their strong points.

9. *Paying Your Own Way*

It may seem like a small point, but a businessman should pay his own way.

In Japan, executive salaries are quite low compared to other countries, especially America. Because of this, it is common to use corporate expense accounts to pad them out. If you are entertaining clients and so on, that's one thing, but in Japan there is also a practice of indulging frequently in what might be called "internal entertainment," which also ends up getting paid with corporate funds. This might involve taking your staff out for a few rounds of drinks, or having a confab over dinner with some colleagues after a meeting.

If the top executives of a company keep sending the tab for such "internal entertainment" to the corporate accountants, it sets a bad example. Many are well aware of this, but do it anyway, because their salaries are so low.

When I became president of Yamato, I gave myself a substantial raise so that I could pay my own way. And in the interests of fairness, I created new standards for compensation of the other corporate officers and sent them to the personnel department for implementation.

This was how I computed them. I first determined what seemed a reasonable differential between the salaries of a newly hired worker and the president of the company, and established a provisional monetary amount for the president's salary—actual take-home pay, after taxes.

The other executives' salaries were then computed in the following manner. For directors who concurrently held administrative positions (for example, serving as both director and general affairs manager) or who had been promoted from administrative positions, I decided a 20 percent salary increase was fair. It might seem a bit low, but as directors they would also receive a larger end-of-the-year bonus, so it seemed OK.

For the senior officers of the company, I first averaged out the monetary amounts of the salaries the other directors with administrative positions were getting after their 20 percent raise, and used this sum as a base figure. I then computed multiples of this amount to arrive at the salaries of the top corporate officers: eight times this amount for a managing director, ten times for a senior managing director, fifteen times for the president of the company.

One problem was that company employees, including those in high administrative posts, were given bonuses twice a year in July and December, while directors were given a single bonus at the end of the fiscal year. In Japan, everybody—even the prime minister!—gets a bonus in July and December, but if the company's bottom line soured sometime afterwards, the directors might wind up getting nothing at all. This was a problem. It wasn't fair if the only reward for being made a director of the company was—nothing. But according to the provisions of Japan's commercial law, directors could receive bonuses only at the end of the fiscal year. This required some ingenuity.

What we decided to do at Yamato Transport was to pay the directors an additional sum of 30 percent over their base salary each month. The personnel department would hold this in escrow for them, and in July and December would give them a lump sum payment for the previous six months (amounting to 1.8 months salary).

Nowadays, more and more companies have moved to an annual salary system, and I think it should be adopted so that this sort of subterfuge is no longer necessary.

In any case, executives should be given the kind of salaries they deserve, and when they want to take their staff drinking they should do it out of their own pocket. If they don't, they had better be prepared never to gain the respect of their employees.

10. High Ethical Standards

If a company is to last, it must have character just as a person has character; and as any person of character has ethical standards, so must the company.

The purpose of a company is to make money, and a company that is turning a profit is a good company; a company that is losing money, no matter how good its products or services may be, is a bad company—or so some people think. In other words, they would have you believe the only reason for a company's existence lies in its ability to generate profits. But is this in fact true?

I don't think so. To my mind, the purpose of a company is continuity. To continue its existence it must generate profit. In other words, profit is both a means and a byproduct of corporate activity.

A corporation is a social entity. It effectively employs capital and assets such as land and machinery, provides goods and services to its region, and helps maintain the standard of living of the country. It also creates employment opportunities in the community and thus supports the lives of the citizens. To do all this the company must maintain the continuity of its activities, and to do that profits are necessary.

I do not think the value of a company to the community would be acknowledged if all its capital came from overseas and all the profits returned there.

To put it in the starkest terms, I think the raison d'être of a corporation is to provide useful goods and services to the community and to support the livelihood of its people by providing them with employment—period. That is what corporate activity is all about. The company should bring happiness to the people of the community, and you could say that this is why it exists in society.

On a personal level, I believe that what is important as a human being is sincerity and compassion. Sincerity and compassion have been my watchwords in dealing with customer and in dealing with employees.

The reason that Yamato Transport, not long after launching Takkyūbin, broke off its relationship with the Mitsukoshi department stores—to whom we owed so much, in a relationship that went back over fifty years to the founding of our company—was because I could no longer condone the total absence of any ethical sense that was displayed by Okada Shigeru, its president at the time. And I vowed to myself then and there that I would never let myself become such a businessman.

Since then, more than twenty years have passed, and thanks to the strong support of our customers and the selfless efforts of our employees, Takkyūbin has developed in a way that we scarcely could have dreamed of in the beginning.

In 1995, the year I was to retire as chairman of the company, we established something called "The Corporate Ideals of Yamato Transport." This was comprised of four elements: "Company Philosophy," "Managerial Ideals," "Corporate Stance," and "Behavioral Guidelines for Employees." I won't go into the details here, but these "Corporate Ideals" stand as guideposts in Yamato's quest to embody high moral and ethical standards as a company, and as a vow to use our Takkyūbin operations to contribute to our community. On an ethical level, they forbid insider trading and corporate contributions, entertainment, or gifts to politicians, and call for attention to environmental concerns. The latter has taken concrete form in the fact that Yamato Transport was the first company in the transport industry to insist that its drivers stop idling their engines when parked or standing—thus reducing emissions and saving precious resources.

I'm only human, and have many faults. But I have always tried to keep sincerity and compassion in mind. A company president may pride himself on his own ethics, but that doesn't produce an ethical company. That takes a strong commitment to ethics on the part of all the employees of the company. But first and foremost, the president must lead the way, setting high goals for everyone to pursue.

Afterword

J apan is now in a major period of transition. Some are calling it the greatest period of change since the Meiji Restoration and Japan's defeat in World War II, and I am inclined to agree. But the Meiji Restoration and World War II transformed politics, law, government, and society, so it was natural that the economy likewise did a 180-degree turn; in the present period of transition, neither the political or governmental systems have altered significantly, and as a result economic change has also been spotty, stopping well short of a radical transformation in most cases.

But the collapse of financial institutions once thought invulnerable has served as the catalyst for a wave of corporate restructuring that has still not spent its force. Corporations and banks of every type and size are all announcing their plans for reorganization.

Restructuring means many different things to many different companies. A number of them overextended themselves during Japan's bubble years, and are now getting rid of unprofitable divisions or operations that have little relationship to the company's core business. This seems long overdue, and not a bad idea. Japanese companies tend to follow the crowd, and many of them start new operations or divisions simply because everybody else seems to be doing it. This kind of imitative behavior rarely succeeds, but it is also characteristic of Japanese firms that once they start down that road, it is difficult to stop—partly as a matter of saving face.

Japanese companies are choked with years of accumulated rust. In many cases they hold on to outdated and useless organizational structures. Since Japanese hate rapid change and like to go slow, reforms are often late in coming even when the need for them is understood. Looked at in this way, the present period of transition offers an excellent chance to companies that are feeling the pinch to carry out reforms. In the name of restructuring to ride out this turbulent period, they can be more thoroughgoing in making necessary changes.

But I think there is also a bad tendency afoot at many companies to use restructuring as an excuse for cutting personnel. After all, a company is a social entity, and employment is its link to the community. It should not fire employees at the drop of a hat—not if it wants to protect the livelihood of the community as a whole.

For an employee, losing a job means losing the foundation of daily life—it is no small thing. If you are going to fire people who have devoted years of their lives to the company, there had better be a very compelling reason for doing so.

From the corporate point of view as well, cutting staff may mean reducing payroll, but don't forget that it also means reducing your fighting strength. In some cases, when reduction of payroll becomes a pressing need, personnel cutbacks may be unavoidable. Yet this should only be resorted to as an emergency measure; it should go without saying that in the long run, it is important for a company to protect the jobs of its workers and increase its competitive strength. Restructuring should cut back on organizational elements that do not contribute directly to revenue, beef up productive lines, and work to invigorate the company from within. If there are to be personnel cuts, they must be done with deliberation, beginning by asking aging officers and executives and people who have been promoted into superfluous positions to step down, and if necessary moving on to encourage employees without families to support to seek employment elsewhere. If care is not exercised in this regard, you can end up with the opposite of what you want, losing your best employees and retaining your most unproductive ones.

If you ask me, the restructuring of our financial institutions has not gone far enough. The reason they have been able to post trillions of yen in extraordinary losses in dealing with the fallout of the bubble era is because they were making such an extraordinary amount of money in the first place. Paying almost zero interest on accounts, jacking up lending rates on loans to struggling companies, and then, when they get in trouble themselves, depending on injections of public funds to maintain their existence—these institutions bear a heavy burden of responsibility for our present economic problems. No wonder their customers are so unhappy.

Before they set about restructuring, the managers of these financial institutions need to make a clear accounting of their own responsibility. I'm not saying they should resign. They should stay on, but do the right thing. Corporate reform is absolutely not a bottom-up process. It can only be accomplished from the top down.

The first thing that needs to be done is to reduce the salaries of people in banking—whose base pay is about 10 percent above that of people in other lines of work. As an expression of apology, they ought to take a pay cut to 10 percent below the norm—20 percent below what they were making when they began relying on public funds to stay in business. I think only an announcement of this sort will make the general public feel that their tax money is not being wasted.

When the postal savings system amassed such huge deposits, the banks complained that this was government interference in what should be private sector business, but they were silenced when postal savings officials asserted that the banks had concentrated their outlets only in major urban areas, while the postal savings network reached everyone, everywhere in the country.

Up to now the restructuring of the banks has involved mergers of city banks, thinning out and consolidation of branch offices, and other measures that put a priority on what is convenient for the banks, while disregarding what might be convenient for their customers. And in fact the distinction between city banks, local banks, and savings and loans is largely an arbitrary creation of the Ministry of Finance. From the standpoint of the user, it is impossible to see why these distinctions are necessary. If you look at it from the standpoint of the needs of the consumer, vertical integration is just as desirable as horizontal integration. But since the world of banking is dominated by a supply-side perspective and lacks an understanding of the consumer's perspective, such changes are unlikely to occur.

In a business world so accustomed to traveling in convoy, the failure of a number of businesses may have been necessary shock treatment—but at this point, it seems not to have had much effect.

I have participated in the management of Yamato Transport for forty-two years. Looking back on it now, what we were doing seems outmoded—analog management, if you will, in what is now a digital age. But I am convinced that in any era, an entrepreneur must have an ethical sense and a feeling of responsibility toward his customers.

In that sense, I think I am fortunate in having done nothing I have been ashamed of in my years as a businessman.

The performance of any company is going to go up and down as time goes on. But I hope from the bottom of my heart that my successors at Yamato will always be able to face the world and continue their journey with their heads held high.

Ogura Masao